Enriching Our Music 2

More Canticles and Settings for the Eucharist

Musical Autography by Music Graphics International

Copyright © 2004 Church Publishing Incorporated

All rights reserved. No part of this book may be reproduced, stored in a retrieval system or transmitted, in any form or by any means, electronic, mechanical, photocopying, recording or otherwise, without the written permission of

Church Publishing Incorporated
19 East 34th Street
New York, NY 10016

Every effort has been made to trace the owner or holder of each copyright. If any rights have been inadvertently infringed upon, the Publisher asks that the omission be excused and agrees to make the necessary corrections in subsequent editions.

ISBN-13: 9780898694444 (paperback)

Preface

During the triennium of 1995-1997 the Standing Commission on Liturgy and Music (SCLM) of the Episcopal Church first met as a newly formed body which combined the previous Standing Liturgical Commission and Standing Commission on Church Music. It was in the discussions of this new commission that the project of producing additional music for the rites of the Book of Common Prayer began to take shape, based on the mandate of a resolution passed by the seventy-first General Convention of 1994. The commission of 2001-2003 reiterated the need for this project to go forward and began collecting materials.

The liturgical supplement *Enriching Our Worship 1* includes texts of revised Eucharistic Prayers and many new canticles. The possibilities for musical settings of these texts became readily apparent, and the SCLM accordingly identified some general areas of need in this regard. For the triennial scope of the project, it seemed practical to focus on mass and canticle settings. Settings for the Eucharist were divided into two categories: through-composed settings of a majority of the ordinary texts (those that form a musical unit as composed by one person and single settings of the ordinary texts. This second collection has been named *Enriching Our Music 2 (EOM2)* and consists of single settings of the ordinary texts of the eucharist; selections that may be used as the hymn of praise or during communion; specific psalms for Morning and Evening Prayer; and two each of Canticles L–S.

The reading committee received several hundred original submissions for *EOM2*. The committee also examined many publications representing a broad variety of denominational resources.

The musical settings in *Enriching Our Music 2* suggest a variety of possibilities for congregations, choirs, and instrumentalists. In addition to their use in the Daily Office and in prayer services, canticles may be included in the Eucharist as the song or hymn of praise when appropriate (see the Book of Common Prayer p. 324 or 356) or on certain occasions in place of the Gradual Psalm, between the Epistle and Gospel, at the Offertory, or during the Communion of the People.

From the beginning, the SCLM envisioned this project to be a musical resource available through print and electronic media. *EOM2* is thus understood to be a musical guide to worship possibilities, note necessarily a volume to serve as a hymnal. Since it is assumed that these congregational materials will be printed in worship leaflets, they will be available electronically. Please refer to www.churchpublishing.org for the source of these electronic products.

We take this opportunity to thank all who submitted their work for this volume. There is no better witness to the ongoing life of our church than these submissions, whether they were ultimately accepted for inclusion or not. Brief notes on those who contributed to this publication may be found at the end of this publication. We are also indebted to the Reading Committee for their diligence, insight and hard work and for the support of Charles Hackman and Larry Reynolds.

Reading Committee

Monte Mason, co-chair
Judith Dodge, co-chair
Albert Melton
Jack Burnam
George Emblom
Ted Yumoto
Sharon Downey

We would also like to thank the Office for Liturgy and Music at the Episcopal Church Center for the innumerable hours of administrative support for this project.

It is with great respect that we acknowledge the guidance and editorial gifts of Marilyn Haskel at Church Publishing concerning this project.

For the Standing Commission on Liturgy and Music,
Monte Mason and Judy Dodge

Notes on the Pointing of the Canticles

The chants in this collection offer an astonishing vitality in form and experimentation even as they are founded in historical chant formulas. A pointing system has been used which provides consistency and accessibility.

Anglican Chant All beginning words are sung to the first note until the / which represents the bar line in the music. Subsequent words or syllables are sung one to each note unless a bracket ⌒ indicates that two or more are to be sung to one note. An underlined word or syllable should be sung to two notes. At the double bar ‖ move to the next line in the text. At the end of some lines, more than one word may need to be sung to the last note. In most cases these are not marked as such.

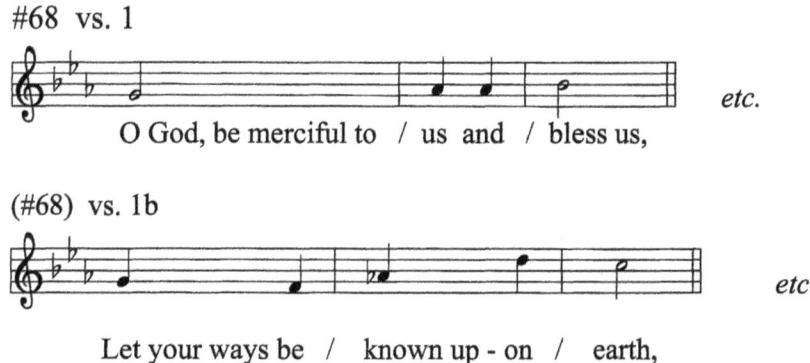

Simplified Anglican Chant Beginning words are sung to the first reciting note until the / which indicates to move to the next note. Subsequently, move to the next note for the next line of text and proceed to the next pitch at the /.

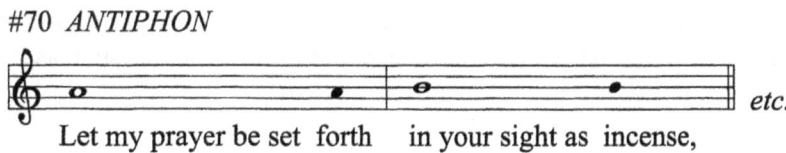

Other styles of chant Beginning words are sung to the first reciting note. At the / move to the next measure. Words in mediant cadences and final cadences (see below) are sung one syllable per note with the following exceptions:

Underlined   great = Sing word or syllable to two notes.

Bracket   God the = Sing multiple words or syllables to one note.

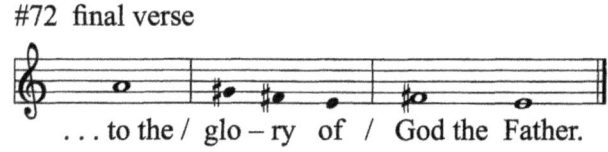

Italics   *I saw* = Sing the italicized word(s) or syllable(s) to the intonation. (see below)

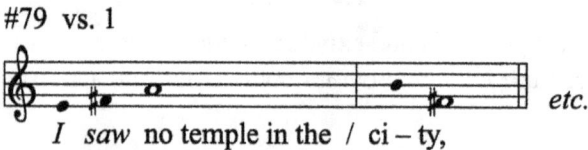

Some cadences may require more than one syllable on the last note. In most cases these are not marked as such.

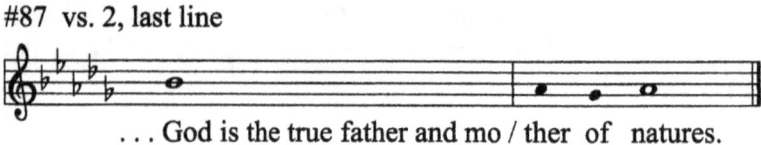

Chant Structure

Punctuation and Breathing in Chant

Breath is always taken at the end of a line and after a colon or semi-colon in the middle of a line. A comma is always observed only as required in good reading and not by a complete break. The word before a comma in the midst of a line may be slightly elongated before continuing on. This, of course, depends on variables such as the length of line, the sense of the text, and space acoustics.

Table of Contents

Opening Acclamation
    MaultsBy   94-96
    Moore
Hymn of Praise
    Bridges   97-103
    Campbell
    Godoy and Martinez
    Hebrew Round
    Praetorius
    Sosa
    Traditional Round
Glory to God
    Chávez-Melo   104, 105
    Crisafulli
Lord, have mercy
    Vasselli   106-114
    MaultsBy
    Boles
    Ferial Mass, XI-XIII c. (Dimmock)
    Hart
    Russian Orthodox
    Emery
    Orr
    Boles
    Dimmock
Holy God
    Giles   116-118
    Morales
    Sanford
Gospel Acclamation
    Caribbean traditional   119-121
    Mozart
    South African
Peace chant
    Giles   122
Eucharistic Prayer 1
    Thomas   123
Holy, holy, holy Lord
    Boles   124-133
    Bridges
    Byzantine
    Chávez-Melo
    Economides
    Garcia
    Godoy and Martinez
    Reza
    Roberto Milano
    Vasselli
Memorial Acclamation
    Dimmock   134-136
    Kucharski
Lord's Prayer
    Godoy and Martinez   137-140
    Hernández
    Mason
    Rimsky-Korsakov

Fraction Anthem
    Averre   **141-148**
    Bianchi
    Chávez-Melo
    Duckworth
    Godoy and Martinez
    Hirten
    Mode 6
    Thomas

Communion
    Berthier   **149-157**
    Hernández
    Roberts
    Shiota

Morning Prayer
    Burdick   **158-161**
    Haskel

Evening Prayer
    Anzalo   **162-167**
    Burdick
    Hurd

Canticles L–S
    Anzalo   **168-180**
    Burdick
    Dimmock
    Emblom
    Hackett
    Haskel
    Hernández
    Martinson
    Mason

Indices
    Title and First Line   *page 141*
    Authors, Composers, Arrangers, Sources   *page 143*
    Biographies of Authors, Composers and Arrangers   *page 145*
    Copyrights   *page 148*

Opening Acclamation: Easter 94

Setting: Hunter Moore, vocal harm. Eric Wyse © 1998 Big Muddy Music.
Used by permission. All rights reserved.

95 Opening Acclamation

Setting: Carl MaultsBy © 2004 Malted Milk Music.
Used by permission. All rights reserved.
You must contact Carl MaultsBy for permission to re-print this setting.

Opening Acclamation II

96

Setting: Carl MaultsBy © 2004 Malted Milk Music.
Used by permission. All rights reserved.
You must contact Carl MaultsBy for permission to re-print this setting.

97 Hymn of Praise *Glory to God*

Glory, glory, unto you, eternal one.
Glory, glory, unto you, eternal one. We
Glory, glory, unto you, eternal one. We

Glory to God - Campbell

Glory to God - Campbell

Setting: William Campbell, from *Service Music Setting No. 2, "A Setting for Peaceful Spitit"* © 1999 William Campbell.
Used by permission. All rights reserved.

Composer Tempo ♩ = ca. 76

Gloria - Godoy & Martinez

Setting: Carlos Mejia Godoy and Pablo Martinez, from *Mass of the Nicaraguan People*, English tr. B. Coult, ed. and arr. R. Lang, S. Schmidt
© 2004 Christ Church Cathedral. Used by permission. All rights reserved.

Composer Tempo ♩ = 66–69

99 — Hymn of Praise *Gloria in excelsis*

Setting: Debra Hinson Bridges © 2004 Debra Hinson Bridges.
Used by permission. All rights reserved.

Hymn of Praise *Gloria, gloria, gloria* 100

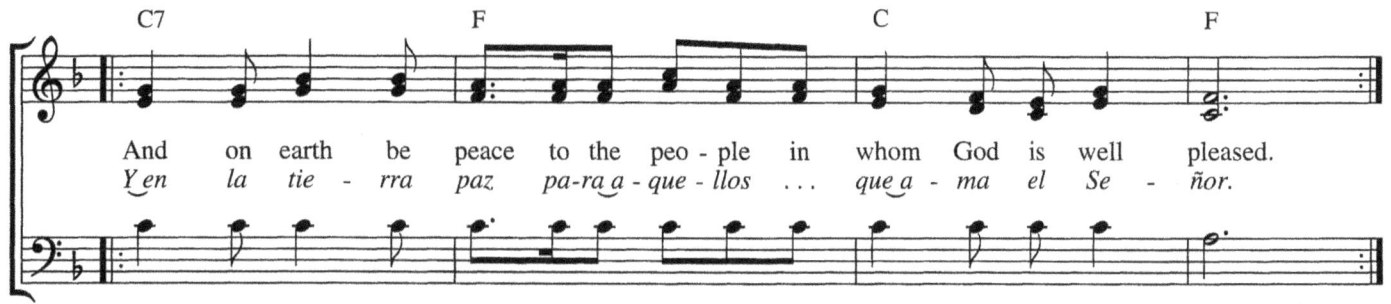

Setting: Pablo Sosa, © 1989 Pablo Sosa. Published by OCP Publications, 5536 NE Hassalo, Portland, OR 97213.
Used by permission. All rights reserved.
You must contact OCP Publications to reproduce this setting.

Hymn of Praise *Jubilate Deo* 101

Setting: Michael Praetorius.

102 Hymn of Praise *Hava Nashirah*

Setting: Hebrew round.

103 Hymn of Praise *Sing and rejoice*

Setting: Traditional round.

Gloria a Dios en el cielo *Glory to God*   104

Gloria a Dios - Chávez-Melo

Gloria a Dios - Chávez-Melo

Gloria a Dios - Chávez-Melo

Gloria a Dios - Chávez-Melo

Setting: Skinner Chávez-Melo, from *Misa Xochipilli* © Juan Francisco Chávez.
Used by permission. All rights reserved.

Gloria - Crisafulli

Gloria - Crisafulli

Gloria - Crisafulli

Setting: Peter Crisafulli, from *Mass Setting for Advent and Christmas* © 2004 Peter Crisafulli

Kyrie for Advent *Lord, have mercy* 106

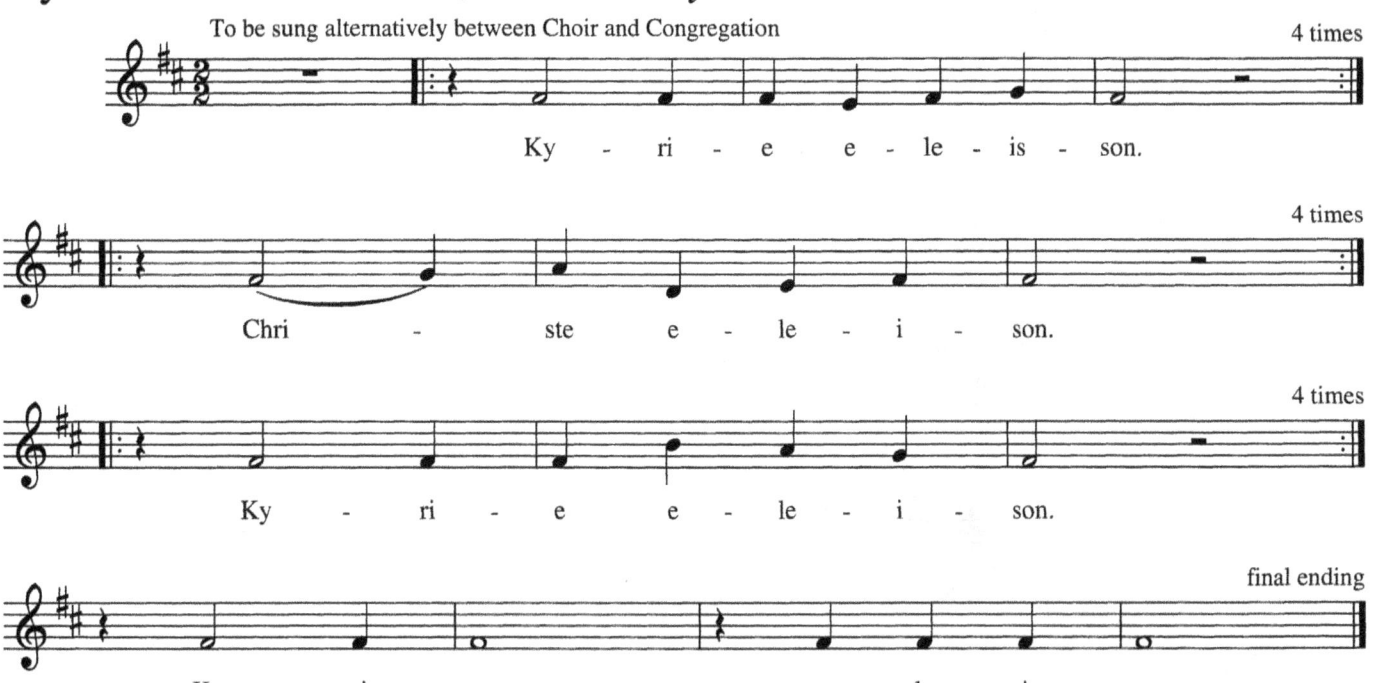

Setting: Stefano Vasselli © 2004 Stefano Vasselli.
Used by permission. All rights reserved.

107 Kyrie for Pentecost *Lord, have mercy*

108   Kyrie eleison *Lord, have mercy*

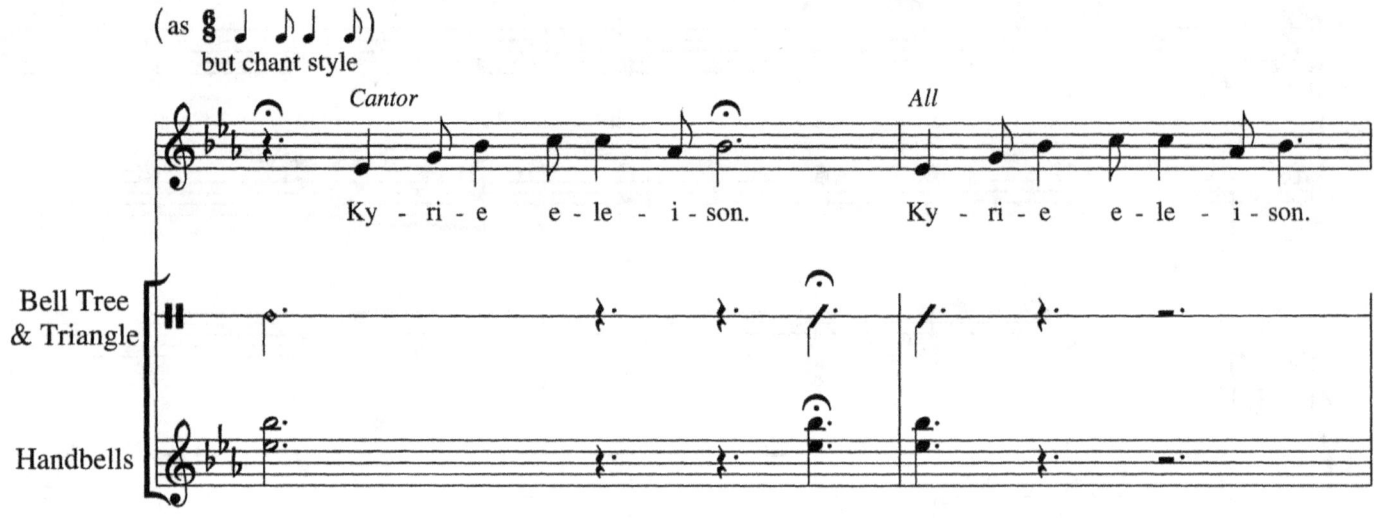
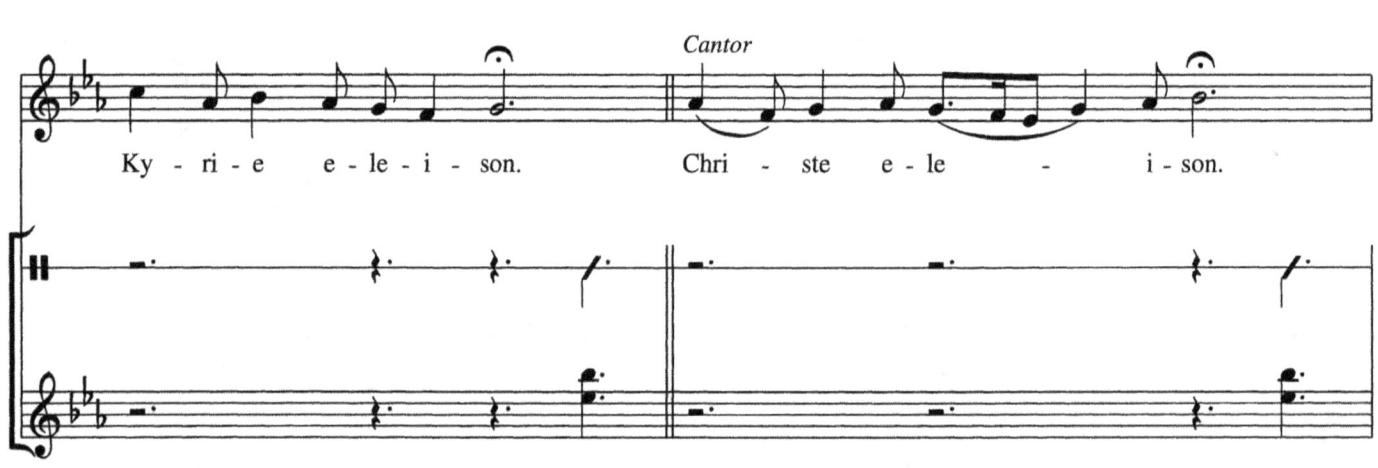
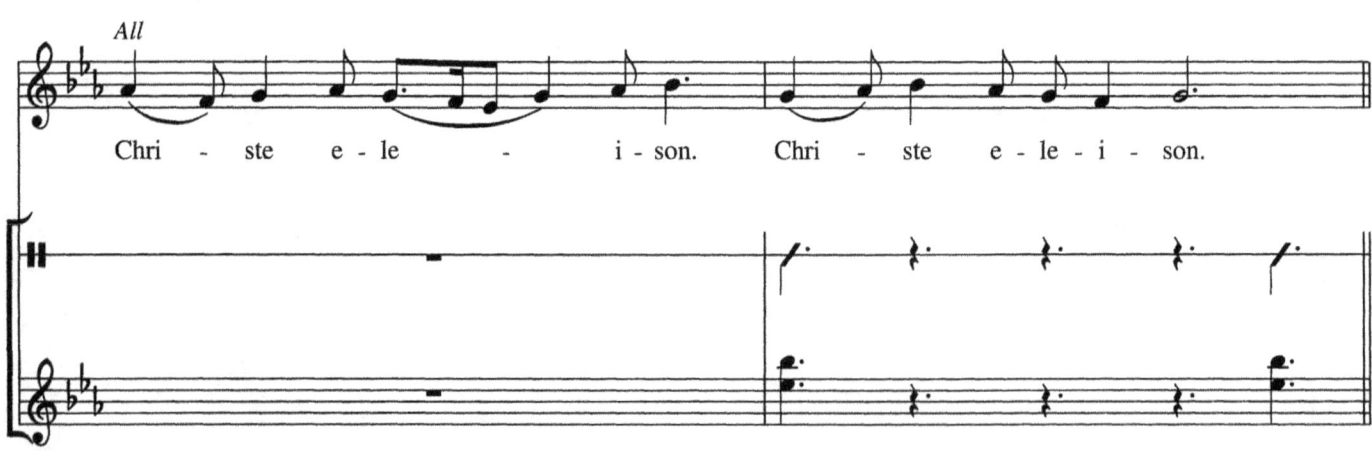

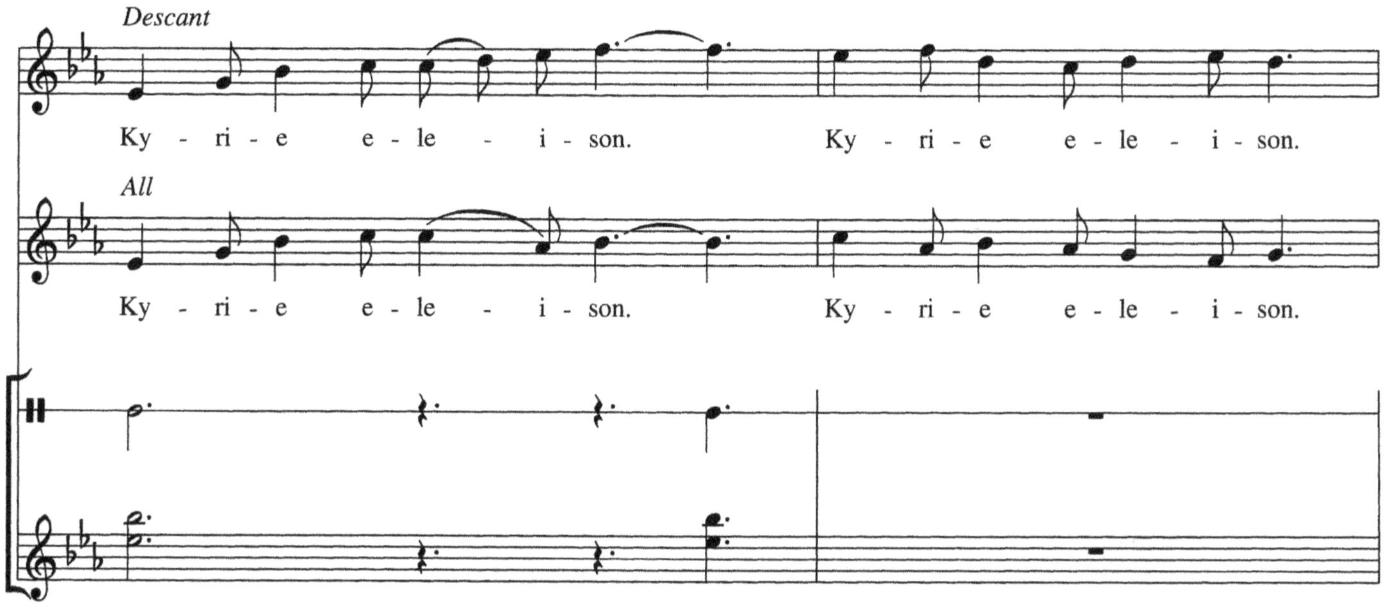

Options: *Handbells doubling at the octave. Add finger cymbals or triangle.*
The cantor part may be sung by one or more voices, either children or adults.

Setting: Frank W. Boles, from *Conditor alme siderum Mass* © 2002 Frank W. Boles.
Used by permission. All rights reserved.

109 Kyrie eleison *Lord, have mercy*

Setting: *Ferial Mass, XI–XIII c.*, arr. Jonathan Dimmock © 2002 Jonathan Dimmock.
Used by permission. All rights reserved.

Kyrie eleison *Lord, have mercy* 110

Setting: Christopher W. Hart © 2004 Christopher W. Hart. Harmonization: Jack Burnam © 2004 Jack Burnam.
Used by permission. All rights reserved.

Kyrie eleison *Lord, have mercy* 111

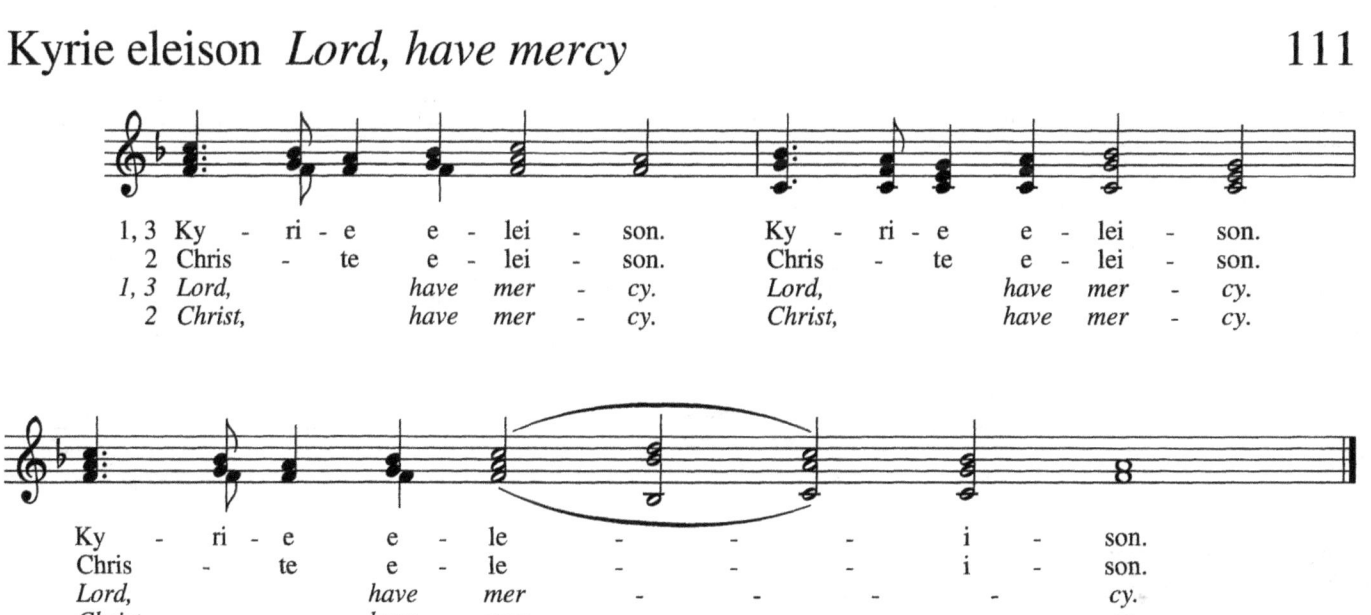

Setting: Russian Orthodox.

112   Lord, have mercy *Kyrie*

Setting: Jane Emery © 2004 Jane Emery.
Used by permission. All rights reserved.

Lord, have mercy *Kyrie eleison* 113

Setting: Philip Orr, from *New Music for Eucharist* © 1994, 2001 Philip Orr.
Used by permission. All rights reserved.

Lord, have mercy *Kyrie eleison*

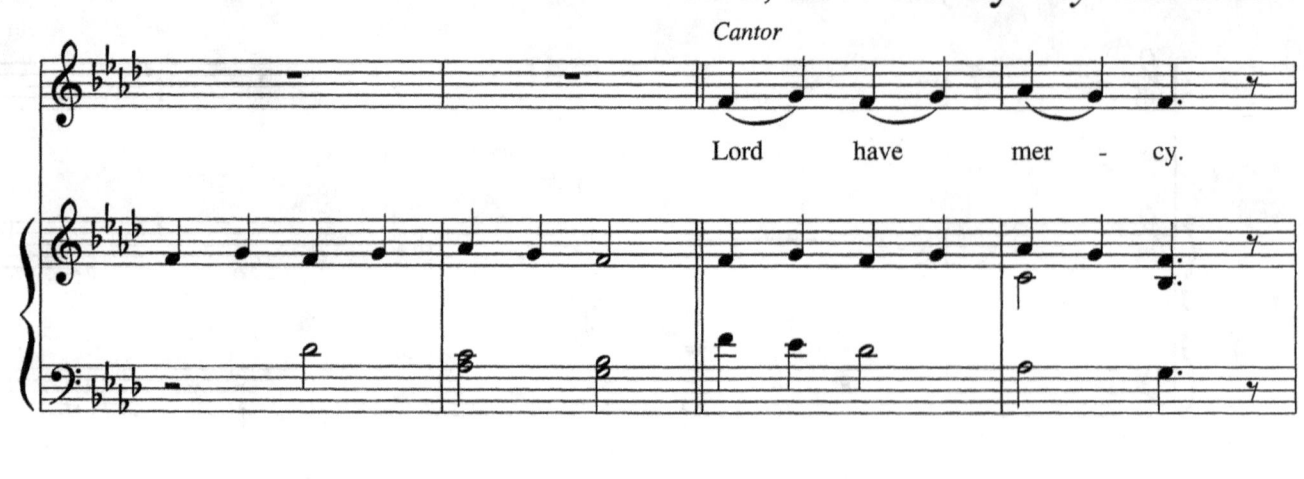

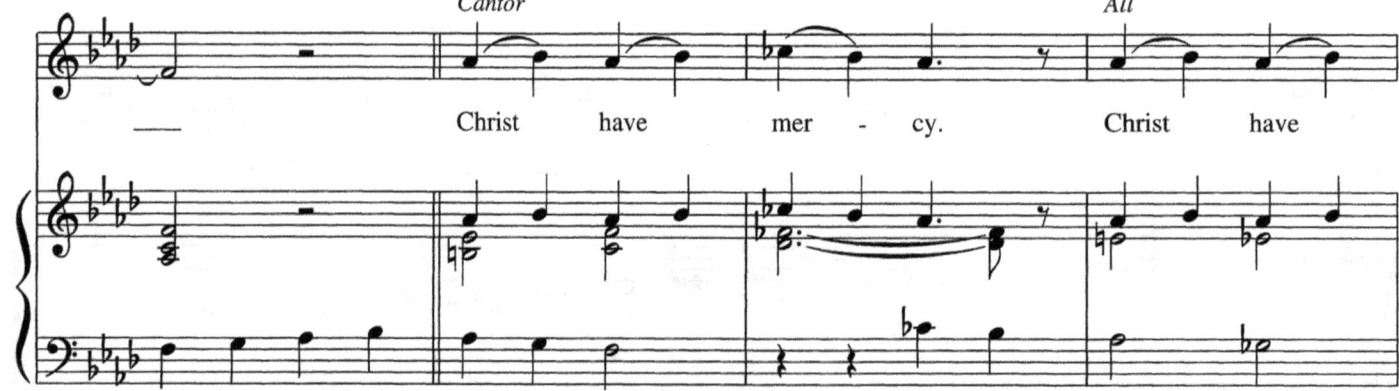

Setting: Frank W. Boles, from *F Minor Service* © 2002 Frank W. Boles.
Used by permission. All rights reserved.

115 Lord, have mercy *Kyrie eleison*

Setting: Jonathan Dimmock, from *St. Ignatius Mass* © 2002 Jonathan Dimmock.
Used by permission. All rights reserved.

Santo, Santo Dios *Trisagion* 116

Setting: Carlos O. Morales © 2004 Carlos O. Morales.
Used by permission. All rights reserved.

117 Hagios, O Theos *Trisagion*

Pronunciation Guide: Hah-ghee-ose oh Thay-ose
Hah-ghee-ose EE-skee-rohs
Hah-ghee-ose ah-thah-nah-tose eh-leh-ee-sohn hee-mahs

Setting: Randall Giles, from Music for the 2002 General Synod of the Church of South India © 2002 Randall Giles.
Used by permission. All rights reserved.

Holy God *Trisagion* 118

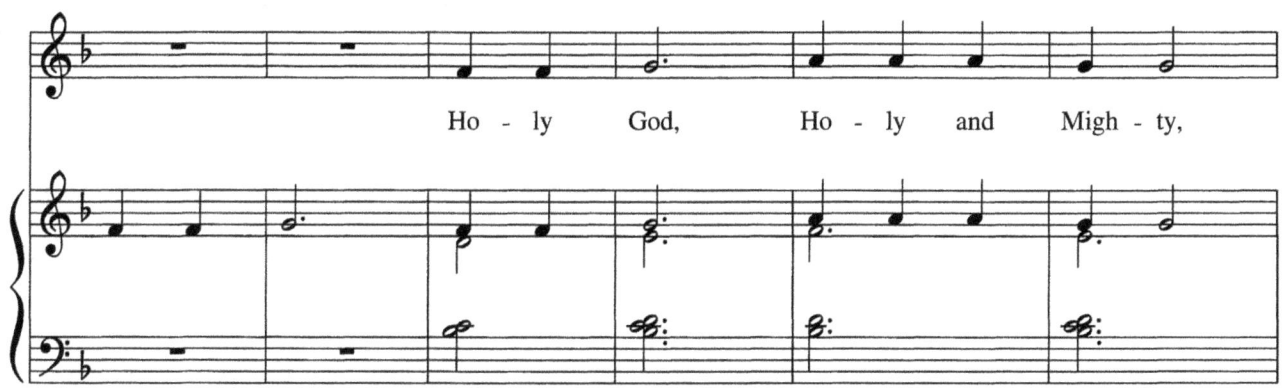

Setting: Melody Galen Sanford; harm. Robert Hawthorne © 2004 Galen Sanford and Robert Hawthorne.
Used by permission. All rights reserved.

119 Halle, Halle, Hallelujah *Gospel Acclamation*

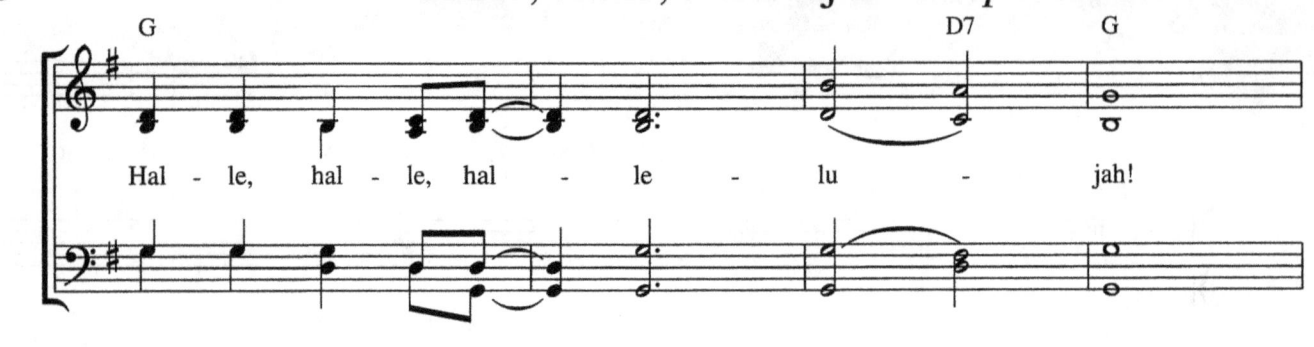

Setting: Caribbean traditional; arr. Mark Sedio © 1995 Augsburg Fortress.
Used by permission. All rights reserved.
You must contact Augsburg Fortress to reproduce this setting.

Alleluia *Gospel Acclamation* 120

Setting: South African, arr. Gobingca Mxadana, 20th cent. © Gobingca Mxadana.
Used by permission. All rights reserved.

Alleluia Canon *Gospel Acclamation* 121

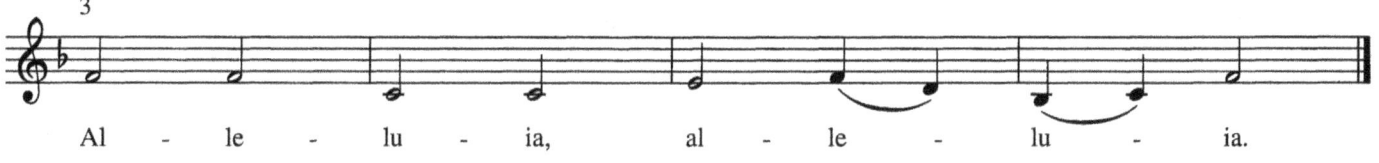

Setting: Adapt. from *Exsultate, Jubilate* by W.A. Mozart (1756–1791).

122   Shanti (Peace)

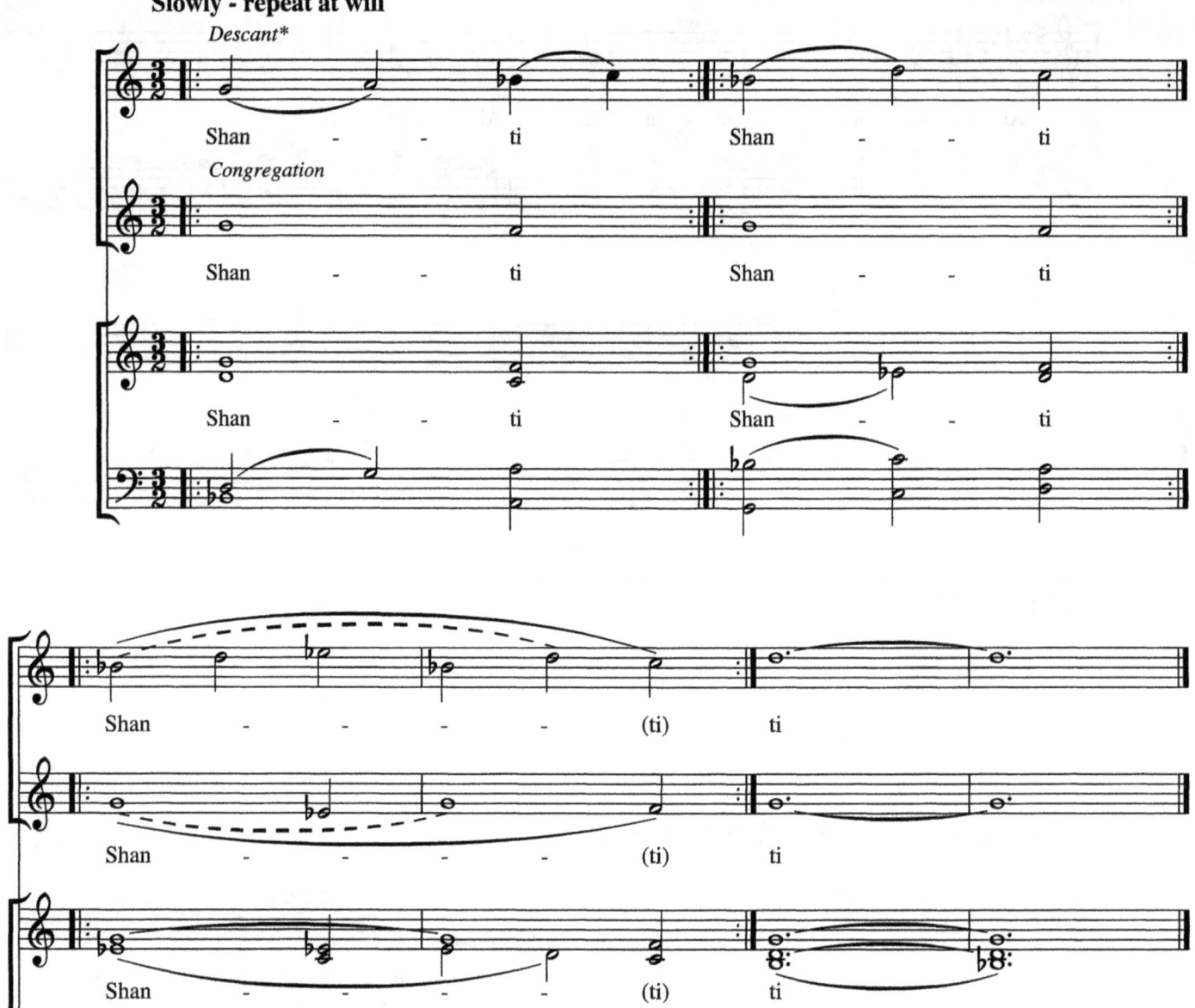

* Descant to appear only after at least two repeats.

Setting: Randall Giles, from Music for the 2002 General Synod of the Church of South India © 2002 Randall Giles.
Used by permission. All rights reserved.

Eucharistic Prayer 1 *Sursum corda and Preface* 123

Setting: Lisa Neufeld Thomas, adapt. from *Missa de Sancta Hildegard* © 2004 Lisa Neufeld Thomas.
Used by permission. All rights reserved.

124   **Sanctus** *Holy, holy, holy Lord*

Sanctus - Bridges

Setting: Debra Hinson Bridges, from *Millennium Mass* © 2004 Debra Hinson Bridges.
Used by permission. All rights reserved.

Composer Tempo ♩ = 100

125   Sanctus *Holy, holy, holy Lord*

Holy, holy, holy Lord - Boles

Handbells may be doubled in octaves. The cantor part may be sung by one or more voices, either children or adults.

Setting: Frank W. Boles, from *Conditor alme siderum Mass* © 2002 Frank W. Boles.
Used by permission. All rights reserved.

126 Holy, holy, holy Lord *Sanctus*

Holy, holy, holy Lord - Economides

Holy, holy, holy Lord - Economides

Holy, holy, holy Lord - Economides

Holy, holy, holy Lord - Economides

Setting: Greg Economides, from *Mass for Theophilus* © 2001 Greg Economides.
Used by permission. All rights reserved.

Composer Tempo ♩ = 212

Holy, holy, holy Lord *Sanctus* 127

Holy, holy, holy Lord - Vasselli

Setting: Stefano Vasselli, from *Mass Setting for Advent and Christmas* © 2004 Stefano Vasselli.
Used by permission. All rights reserved.

Throughout a life of hardship *Sanctus*

128

Throughout a life of hardship - Goday & Martinez

Setting: Carlos Mejia Godoy and Pablo Martinez, from *Mass of the Nicaraguan People,* English tr. B. Coult, ed. and arr. R. Lang, S. Schmidt
© 2004 Christ Church Cathedral. Used by permission. All rights reserved.

Composer Tempo ♩ = 92–96

129 Santo *Holy, holy, holy Lord*

Setting: Juan Luis Garcia © Estate of Juan Luis Garcia.
Used by permission. All rights reserved.

Page has been left blank
to facilitae page turns

130 Santo *Holy, holy, holy Lord*

Holy, holy, holy Lord - Chávez-Melo

Setting: Skinner Chávez-Melo, from *Misa Xochipilli* © Juan Francisco Chávez.
Used by permission. All rights reserved.

131   Santo *Holy, holy, holy Lord*

Setting: Mary F. Reza; arr. Joseph H. Abell © 1996 Mary F. Reza and Joseph H. Abell.
Used by permission. All rights reserved.

Santo *Holy, holy, holy Lord* 132

Setting: Roberto Milano © Roberto Milano.
Used by permission. All rights reserved.

133   Holy, holy, holy Lord

Best when sung unaccompanied. Lines 3 and 5 may also be sung by cantor alone.

Setting: Byzantine; adapt. George Black © 2004 George Black.
Used by permission. All rights reserved.

Memorial Acclamation *Christ has died* 134

Setting: Joseph A. Kucharski, from *Mass in Honor of St. Anthony* © 2004 Joseph A. Kucharski.
Used by permission. All rights reserved.

135   **Memorial Acclamation** *Dying you destroyed our death*

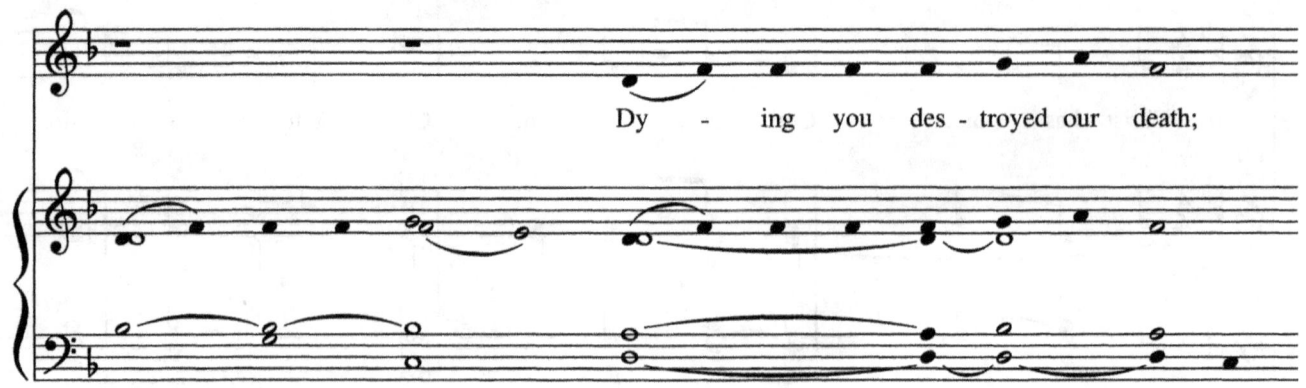

Setting: Jonathan Dimmock, from *St. Ignatius Mass* © 2002 Jonathan Dimmock.
Used by permission. All rights reserved.

136   **Memorial Acclamation** *Christ has died*

Setting: Jonathan Dimmock, from *St. Ignatius Mass* © 2002 Jonathan Dimmock.
Used by permission. All rights reserved.

138   Lord's Prayer *Our Father in heaven*

Setting: Nicholas Rimsky-Korsakov (1844–1908); arr. George Black © 2004 George Black.
Used by permission. All rights reserved.

The Lord's Prayer *Our Father in heaven* 139

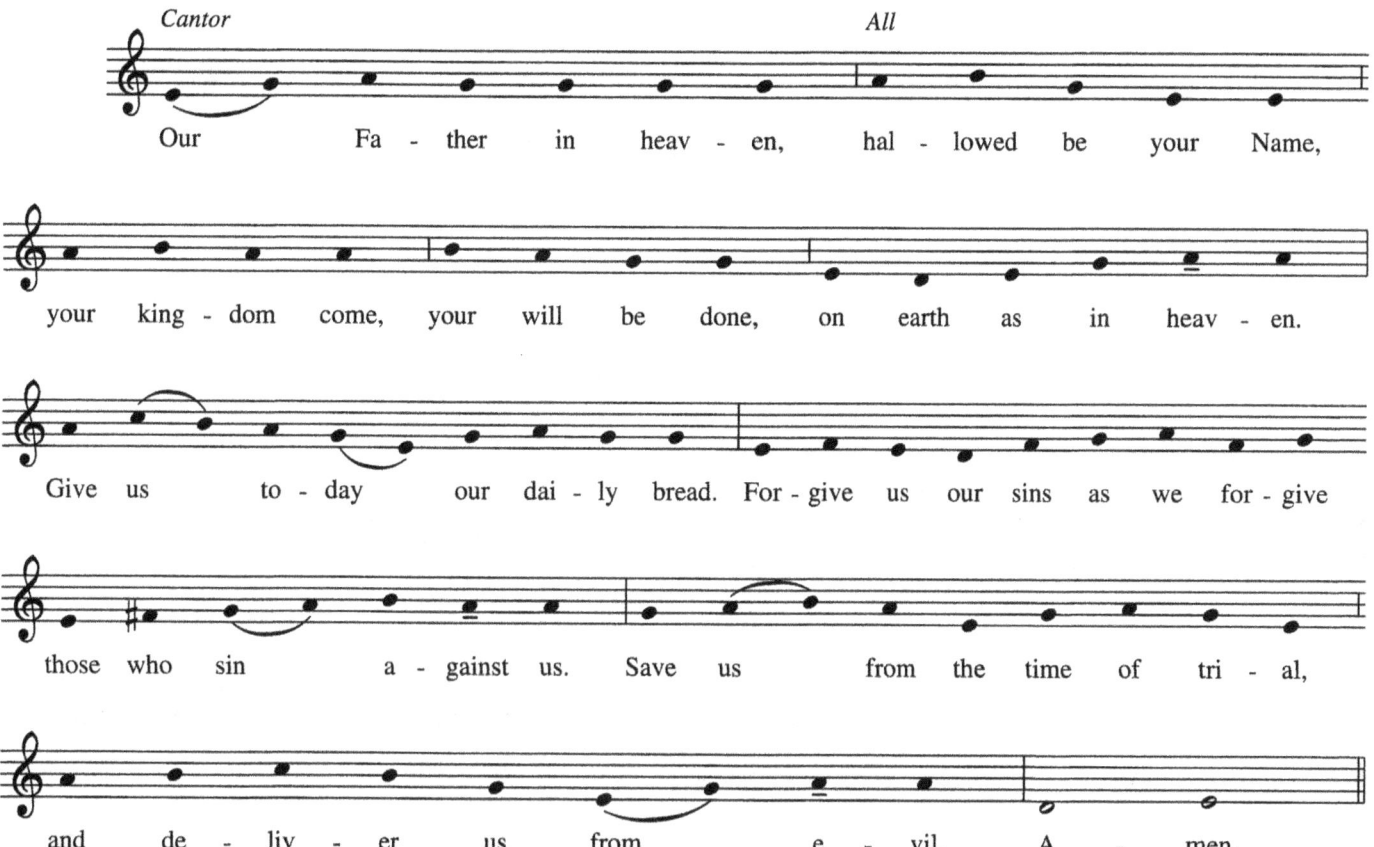

Setting: Monte Mason © 2004 Monte Mason.
Used by permission. All rights reserved.

Eternal Spirit

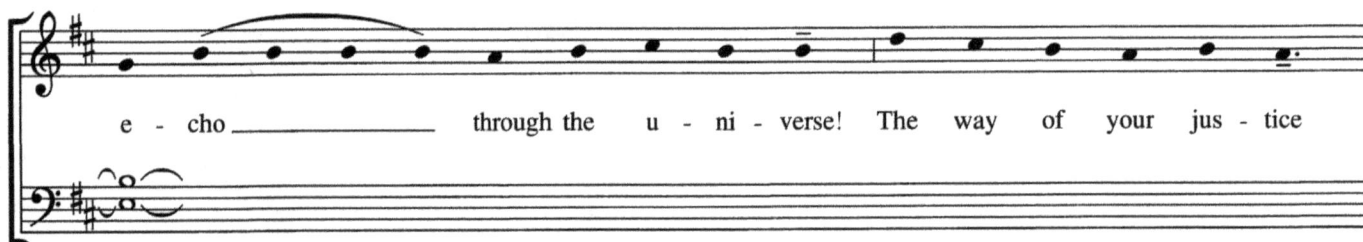

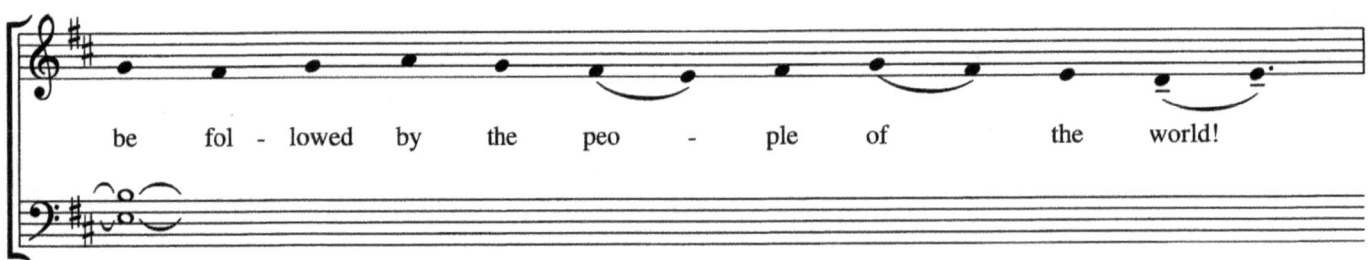

Eternal Spirit - Hernández

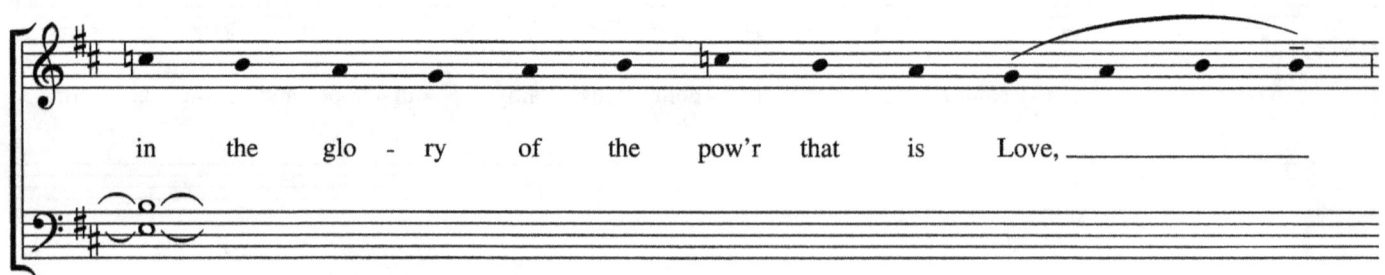

This should be sung at a pitch comfortable for the singer(s). Any drone may be used; Additional pitches may be added to the drone, such as D♯ and F♯, which may be brought in and out randomly to alter the texture.

Words: Jim Cotter © 1989 Church of the Province of New Zealand.
Music: Ana Hernández © 1994 Ana Hernández.
Used by permission. All rights reserved.

Fraction Anthem *Christ our Passover* 141

Setting: Bonnie Duckworth © 2004 Bonnie Duckworth.
Used by permission. All rights reserved.

142   Fraction Anthem *Lamb, O Lamb of God*

Setting: Carlos Mejia Godoy and Pablo Martinez, from *Mass for the Nicaraguan People*, English tr. B. Coult, ed. and arr. R. Lang, S. Schmidt
© 2004 Christ Church Cathedral. Used by permission. All rights reserved.

143 Fraction Anthem *Lamb of God*

Lamb of God - Hirten

Setting: John Karl Hirten © 2004 John Karl Hirten.
Used by permission. All rights reserved.

Composer Tempo ♩ = 76

144   Lamb of God *Agnus Dei*

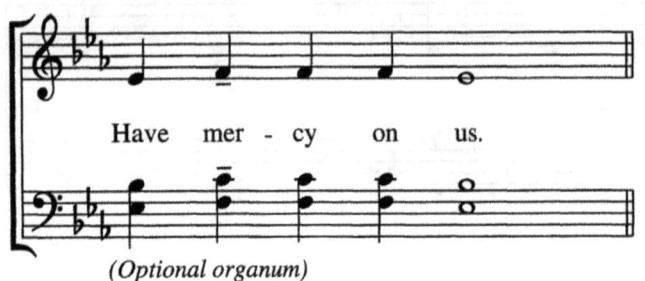

(Optional organum)

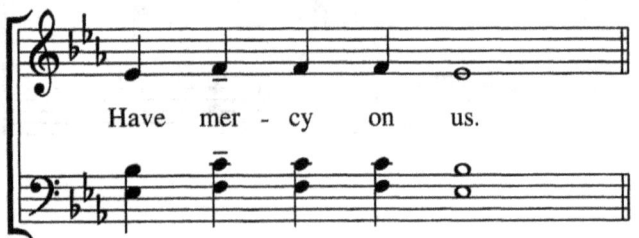

Setting: Lisa Neufeld Thomas, adapt. from *Missa de Sancta Hildegard* © 1997 Lisa Neufeld Thomas.
Used by permission. All rights reserved.

Fraction Anthem *Cordero de Dios* 145

Setting: Vicente Bianchi © Vicente Bianchi.
Used by permission. All rights reserved.

146 Fraction Anthem *Cordero de Dios*

Setting: Skinner Chávez-Melo, from *Misa Xochipilli* © Juan Francisco Chávez.
Used by permission. All rights reserved.

Fraction Anthem *We who are many* 147

Setting: Mode 6, based on *Ubi caritas*, adapt. David Hurd © 1998 David Hurd.
Used by permission. All rights reserved.

148   **Fraction Anthem** *Be known to us*

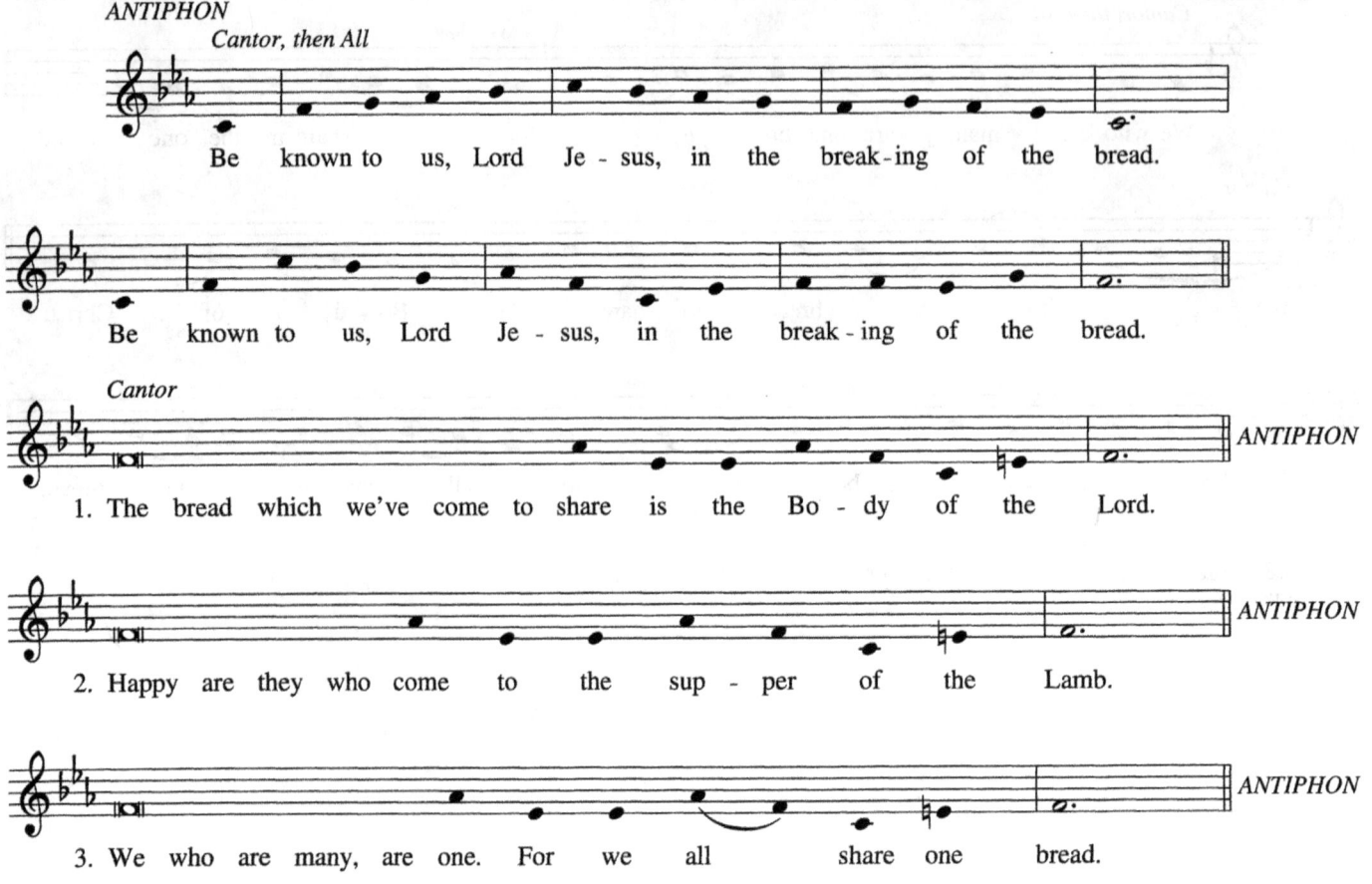

Setting: Richard E. Averre © 2004 Richard E. Averre.
Words: Frank T. Griswold © 2004 Frank T. Griswold.
Used by permission. All rights reserved.

Ubi caritas 149

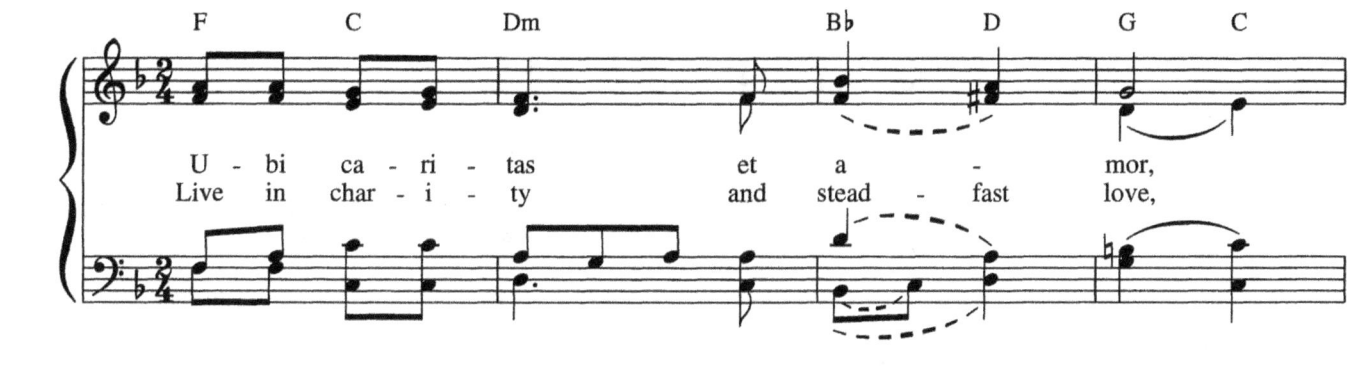

Ubi caritas et amor, ubi caritas Deus ibi est.
Live in charity and steadfast love, live in charity; God will dwell with you.

Setting: Jacques Berthier, from *Songs and Prayers from Taizé* © 1991 by Les Presse de Taizé (France).
Used by permission of GIA Publications, Inc. 7404 S. Mason Avenue, Chicago, IL 60638. www.giamusic.com. 800-442-1358. All rights reserved.
You must contact GIA Publications to reproduce this setting.

Kirisuto no heiwa *The Peace of Christ* 150

Kirisuto no heiwa ga watashi tachi no kokoro no sumi-zumi ni made yuki watarimasu yoni
hikari
chikara
inochi

Translation: May the peace (light, power, life) of Christ fill up every corner of our hearts.
Pronunciation guide: Kee-ree-soo-toh noh hey-ee-wah gah
wah-tah-shee tah-chee noh ko-koh-ro noh
soo-mee-zoo-mee-nee mah-deh
yoo-kee wah-tah-ree ma-soo yoh-nee
hee-kah-ree
chee-kah-rah
ee-noh-chee

Words and Music: Izumi Shiota © Izumi Shiota.
Used by permission. All rights reserved.

151 Be still and know

Be still and know - Hernandez

The part numbered 1 should be sung alone and repeated several times. Then the parts numbered 2, 3, and 4 are added one at a time repeating each new group several times before the next part enters. There is no end to the tune, and you may continue as long as forever, or bring the parts out in reverse order for a tidier finish.

Words: Ana Hernández © Ana Hernández.
Music: Ana Hernández, *Meditation No. 9*, © Ana Hernández
All rights reserved. Used by permission.

Composer Tempo ♩ = 80

152 — You are beloved Canticle N (paraphrase)

You are beloved - Hernandez

Begin with ATB parts sung together. Then add Drone *and* St. Columba *after successive repeats.*
This selection may be sung at a pitch comfortable for the singers.

Setting: Ana Hernández, *Meditation No. 10*, © 2002 Ana Hernández
Used by permission. All rights reserved.

153 God, to my words encline thine ear

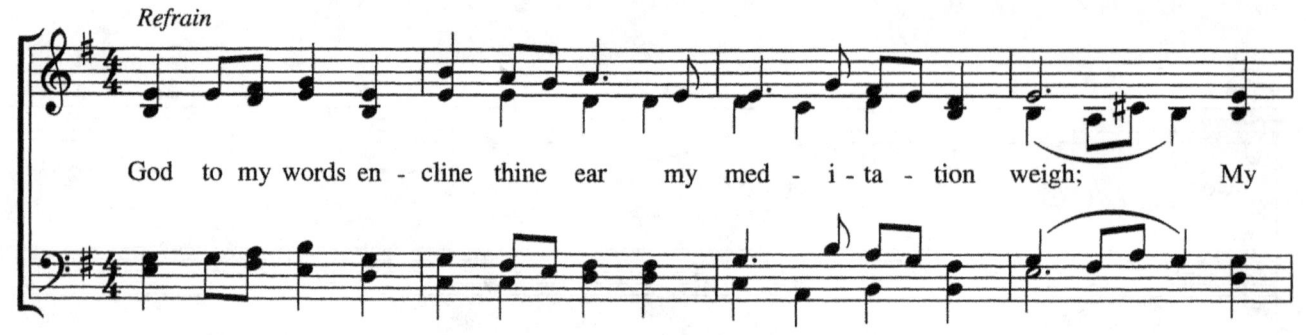
God to my words en-cline thine ear my med-i-ta-tion weigh; My

Sov-reign strong vouch-safe to hear my cry to thee, I pray.

Accompaniment to verses

Hmmm

God, to my words encline thine ear - Robert

1. God in th'a-bun-dance of thy Grace will I draw near:
And t'ward thy most Ho-ly place will wor-ship thee in fear.

2. For God doth right-eous folk es-teem, and them for ev-er bless. God's fa-vour shall en-com-pass them, a shield in their dis-tress.

3. Yea, shout for joy for ev-ver-more, pro-tect-ed still by thee:
Let them that do thy name a-dore in that still joy-ful be.

Words: *Psalm V* paraphrase by George Herbert, alt. William Bradley Roberts.
Music: William Bradley Roberts © 1995 William Bradley Roberts.
Used by permission. All rights reserved.

O come to my heart, Lord Jesus - Roberts

Words: Emily Elizabeth Steele Elliott, 1864.
Music: William Bradley Roberts © 2000 William Bradley Roberts.
Used by permission. All rights reserved.

155 Christ, my hope, and Christ, my joy

Refrain may be sung repeatedly after last verse or verses may be omitted, repeating refrain as a mantra.

Christ, my hope, and Christ, my joy - Roberts

1. We are come to your table, God, to see you face to face; in your presence is fullest joy, in your life is surest hope. *D.C.*

2. Our faith is in you, our trust is in your Word; O God, we believe; come help our unbelief. *D.C.*

3. In you we find our strength, in you we find our light; O give us courage, God, to live our lives in you. *D.C.*

Words: Refrain, tr. from German by William Bradley Roberts; verses by William Bradley Roberts © 1994 William Bradley Roberts.
Music: Refrain, Catalon folksong from Taizé; arr. William Bradley Roberts © 1994 William Bradley Roberts.
Used by permission. All rights reserved.

156 — My spirit is longing

My spirit is longing for you, my God; my spirit is waiting in hope. My spirit is longing for you, my God; my spirit is waiting in hope.

Words and Music: William Bradley Roberts © 1994 William Bradley Roberts.
Used by permission. All rights reserved.

Christ is arisen! Hallelujah! 157

Christ is a-ris-en! Hal-le-lu-jah! He has be-come our sal-va-tion!

1. The Lord is my Light and my sal-vation;
2. One thing have I asked of the Lord; one thing I seek;
3. For in the day of trouble he shall keep me safe in his shelter;

whom then shall I fear?
that I may dwell in the house of the Lord all the days of my life;
he shall hide me in the secrecy of his dwelling, and set me high up-on a rock.

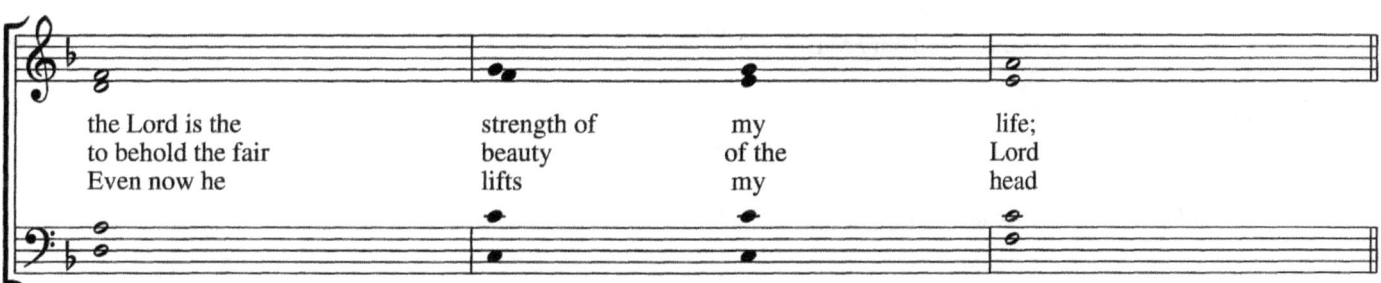

the Lord is the strength of my life;
to behold the fair beauty of the Lord
Even now he lifts my head

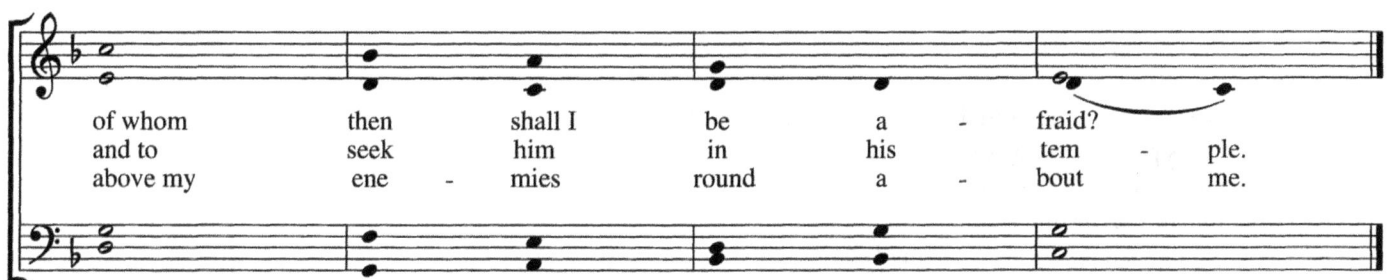

of whom then shall I be a-fraid?
and to seek him in his tem-ple.
above my ene-mies round a-bout me.

Words: *Psalm 27:1, 5–8.*
Music: William Bradley Roberts © 2000 William Bradley Roberts.
Used by permission. All rights reserved.

158 Venite *Psalm 95:1–7*

Come, let us / sing to the / Lord;
    let us shout for joy to the / Rock of / our sal / vation.
Let us come before God's / presence with thanks / giving
    and raise to the / Lord a / shout with / psalms.

For you are a / <u>great</u> / God;
    you are / great a / bove all / gods.
In your hand are the / caverns of the / earth,
    and the heights of the / hills are / <u>yours</u> / also.

†The sea is / yours, for you / made it,
    and your hands have / molded the / <u>dry</u> / land.

Come, let us bow down and / bend the / knee,
    and kneel be / fore the / Lord our / Maker.
For your are our God,
and we are the people of your pasture and the / sheep of your / hand.
Oh, that today we would / hearken / to your / voice!

The following verses are added when Psalm 95 is used as the Invitatory:

Harden not your hearts,
    as your forebears / did in the / wilderness,
    at Meribah, and on that day at / Massah, / when they / tempted me.
They put me / to the / test,
    though / they had / seen my / works.

Forty years long I detested that gene / ration and / said,
    "This people are wayward in their hearts;
    they / do not / know my / ways."
So I / swore in my / wrath,
    "They shall not / enter / into my / rest."

Setting: Owen Burdick © 2004 Owen Burdick.
Used by permission. All rights reserved.

Page has been left blank
to facilitae page turns

159 Venite: *Psalm 95:1–7*

Come, let us sing / to the Lord;
    let us shout for joy to the Rock of / our salvation.
Let us come before God's presence / with thanksgiving
    and raise to the Lord a / <u>shout</u> with psalms.

For you are a / <u>great</u> God;
    you are great a / bove all gods.
In your hand are the caverns / of the <u>earth</u>,
    and the heights of the / hills are yours also.

The sea is yours, / for you made it,
    and your hands have mold / ed the dry land.
Come, let us bow down and / bend the <u>knee</u>,
    and kneel before the / <u>Lord</u> our Maker.

For you / are our God,
    and we are the people / of your pasture
    and the sheep / of your <u>hand</u>.
Oh, that today we would / he͡arken to your voice!

The following verses are added when Psalm 95 is used as the Invitatory:
A cantor or small group monotones the text on E. The accompaniment
moves to the next chord on the underlined words.

<u>Let</u> us listen today to God's voice:
<u>Harden</u> not your hearts,
as your <u>forebears</u> did in the wilderness,
    at Meribah, and on that <u>day</u> at Massah,
    when they <u>tempted</u> me.
<u>They</u> put me to the test,
    though they had seen my works.

Venite - Haskel

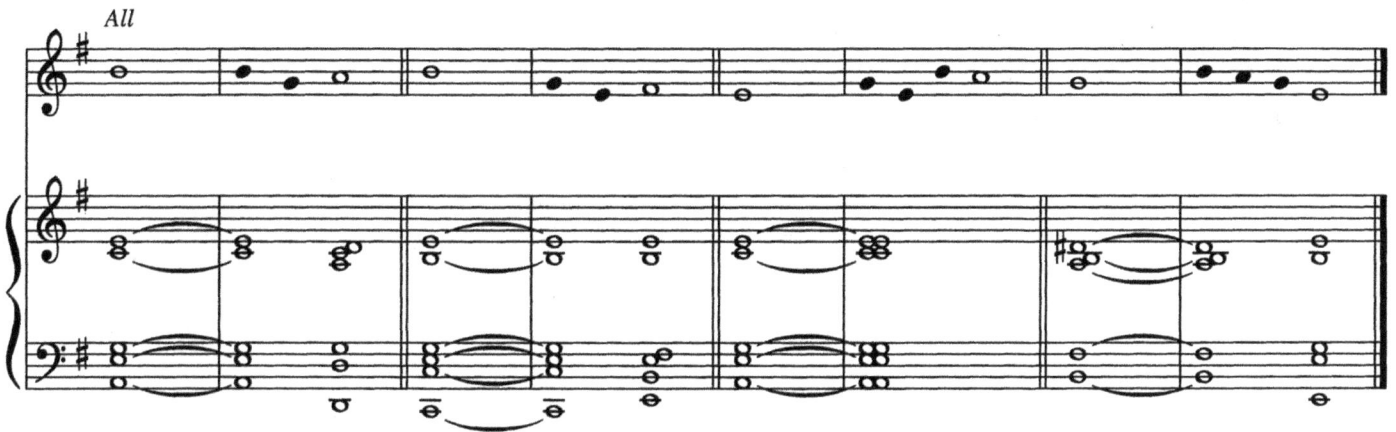

Forty years long I detested that genera / tion and said,
    "This people are wayward / in their hearts;
    they do not / know my ways."
So I swore in my wrath,
"They shall not enter / into my rest."

Setting: Marilyn Haskel, harm. Dorothy J. Papadakos © 2004 Marilyn Haskel.
Used by permission. All rights reserved.

160   Psalm 63:1–8 *O God, you are my God (morning)*

ANTIPHON
Cantor, then all

O God, you are my God; from break of day I seek you.

O God, you are my God; / eagerly I / seek you;
   my soul thirsts for you, my flesh faints for you,
      as in a barren and dry land / where there / is no / water.
Therefore I have gazed upon you in your / holy / place,
   that I might / behold your / power and your / glory.   **ANTIPHON**

For your loving-kindness is better than / life it / self;
   my / lips shall / give you / praise.
So will I bless you as / long as I / live
   and lift up my / hands / in your / Name.   **ANTIPHON**

My soul is content, as with / marrow and / fatness,
   and my mouth praises / you with / joyful / lips,
When I remember you up / on my / bed,
   and meditate on / you in the / night / watches.   **ANTIPHON**

For you have / been my / helper,
   and under the shadow of your / wings I / will re / joice.
My soul / clings to / you;
   Your / right hand / holds me / fast.   **ANTIPHON**

Setting: Owen Burdick © 2004 Owen Burdick.
Used by permission. All rights reserved.

Psalm 67:1–5 *O God, be merciful to us (morning)*   161

ANTIPHON

Day by day we bless you; we praise your name for-ev-er-more.

Verse 1 and 2

Verse 3

O God, be merciful to / us and / bless us,
    show us the light of your / coun-te / nence and / come to us.
Let your ways be / known up-on / earth,
    your saving / health a / mong all / nations.   **ANTIPHON**

Let the peoples / praise you, O / God;
    let / all the / peoples / praise you.
Let the nations be glad and / sing for / joy,
    for you judge the peoples with equity
    and guide all the / nations / upon / earth.   **ANTIPHON**

Let the peoples / praise you, O / God;
    let / all the / peoples / praise you.   **ANTIPHON**

Setting: Owen Burdick © 2004 Owen Burdick.
Used by permission. All rights reserved.

162 Psalm 134 *Behold now, bless the Lord (evening)*

May be sung in unison or harmony.

Setting: Raul Anzalo © 2004 Raul Anzalo.
Used by permission. All rights reserved.

Psalm 141:1-3, 8ab *O Lord, I call to you (evening)* 163

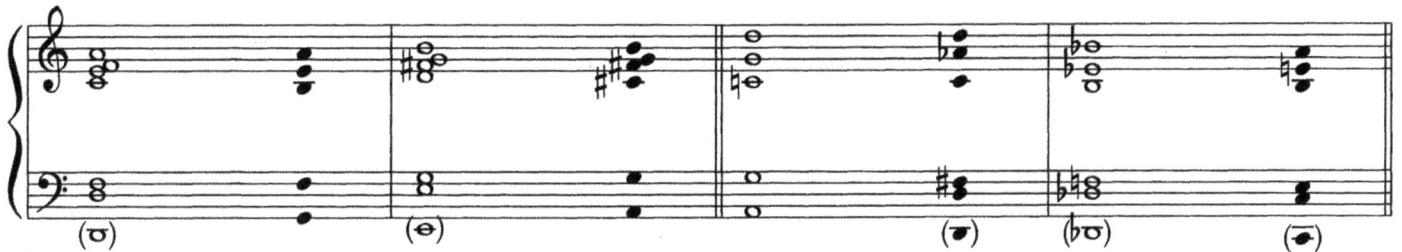

ANTIPHON
Let my prayer be set / forth
in your sight as / incense,
    the lifting up of my / hands
    as the evening / sacrifice.

O Lord, I call to you; come to me / quickly;
    hear my voice when I cry to / you.
Let my prayer be set forth in your sight as / incense,
    the lifting up of my hands as the evening / sacrifice.

Set a watch before my mouth, O Lord,
and guard the door of my / lips;
    let not my heart incline to any evil / thing.
My eyes are turned to you, Lord / God;
    in you I take / refuge.

In the seasons of Advent, Christmas, Lent, and Easter, and on Holy Days, antiphons drawn from the opening sentences given in the Offices or from other passages of Scripture, may be used instead. The Phos hilaron may be sung to this chant as well.

Setting: Owen Burdick © 2004 Owen Burdick.
Used by permission. All rights reserved.

164

Now, Lord, you let your servant go in peace

165 Canticle L: *A Song of Christ's Humility*

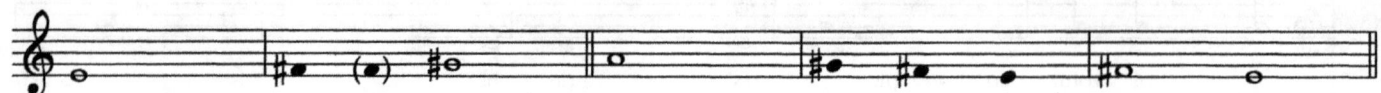

Though in the form / of God,
    Christ Jesus did not cling to e / quality / with God,

But emptied himself, taking the form of a / servant,
    and was born / in human / likeness.

Being found in human form, he humbled / himself
    and became obedient to death, even / death on a / cross.

Therefore, God has highly exalt / ed him
    and given him the / name above / every name,

That at the name of Jesus, every knee / shall bow,
    in heaven and on earth and / under the / earth,

And every tongue confess that Jesus Christ / is Lord,
    to the / glory of / God the Father.

Setting: Monte Mason from the Orthodox Church © 2004 Monte Mason.
Used by permission. All rights reserved.

Canticle L *A Song of Christ's Humility*

A Song of Christ's Mercy - Burdick

A Song of Christ's Mercy - Burdick

The left hand accompaniment should be soft throughout (celestes or light foundations). The right hand might be a bit louder with perhaps a soft reed (oboe) to help lead the congregation. The pedal should use soft 16' & 8' stops. When performed as a solo, transpose up to a minor third higher, a piacere.

A piano version in this key and a solo version for Soprano or Tenor in G Major are available from the composer

Setting: Owen Burdick © 2004 Owen Burdick
Used by permission. All rights reserved.

Composer Tempo ♩ = 63

167 Canticle M: *A Song of Faith*

Blessed be the God and Father of our Lord Jesus / Christ,
    by divine mercy we have a new birth into a living / hope;
Through the resurrection of Jesus Christ from the / dead,
    we have an inheritance that is imperishable in / heaven.

The ransom that was paid to / free us
    was not paid in silver or / gold,
But in the precious blood of / Christ,
    the Lamb without spot or / stain.

†God raised Jesus from the dead and gave him / glory
so that we might have faith and hope in / God.

* *omit at end*
† *second half*

Setting: George Emblom © 2004 George Emblom.
Used by permission. All rights reserved.

Canticle M: *A Song of Faith*   168

Blessed be the God and Father of our Lord / Jesus Christ,
    by divine mercy we have birth into a / living hope;

Through the resurrection of Jesus Christ / from the dead,
    we have an inheritance that is imperishable / in heaven.

The ransom that was paid / to free us
    was not paid in sil / ver or gold.

But in the precious / blood of Christ,
    the Lamb without / spot or stain.

God raised Jesus from the dead and gave / him glory
    so that we might have faith and / hope in God.

Setting: Monte Mason © 2004 Monte Mason.
Used by permission. All rights reserved.

A Song of God's Love - Anzalo

5. Be-lov-ed, since God loved us so much, we ought also to love one an-oth-er.

6. For if we love one another, God abides in us, and God's love will be perfec-ted in us.

Setting: Raul Anzalo © 2004 Raul Anzalo.
Used by permission. All rights reserved.

170 Canticle N: *A Song of God's Love*

A Song of God's Love - Haskel

171   Canticle O: *A Song of the Heavenly City*

A Song of the Heavenly City - Mason

A Song of the Heavenly City - Mason

* Optional ending: skip next four measures and continue from **. May be played by any combination of instruments (organ, other keyboard, handbells).

Setting: Monte Mason © 2001 Monte Mason.
Used by permission. All rights reserved.

172　Canticle O: *A Song of the Heavenly City*

I saw no temple in the / city,
　　for its temple is the God of surpassing strength / and the <u>Lamb</u>.

And the city has no need of sun or moon to / light it,
　　for the glory of God shines on it, and its lamp / is the <u>Lamb</u>.

By its light the nations shall / <u>walk</u>,
　　and the rulers of the world lay their honor / and glory there.

Its gates shall never be shut by day, nor shall there be any / <u>night</u>;
　　into it they will bring the honor and glo / ry of nations.

I saw the clean river of the water of life, bright as / crystal,
　　flowing from the throne of God and / of the <u>Lamb</u>.

The tree of life spanned the river, giving fruit every / <u>month</u>,
　　and the leaves of the tree were for the heal / ing of nations.

All curses cease where the throne of God and the Lamb stands,
and all servants give worship / <u>there</u>;
　　there they will see God's face, whose Name shall / be on their foreheads.

After the first verse, the intonations may be omitted, thus beginning on the reciting note.

Setting: Monte Mason © 2004 Monte Mason.
Used by permission. All rights reserved.

Canticle P: *A Song of the Spirit* 173

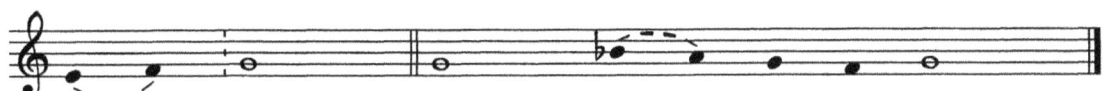

"*Behold*, I am coming soon," says the Lord,
"and bringing my reward with me,
  to give to everyone ac / cording to their deeds.

"*I am* the Alpha and the Omega, the first and the last,
  the be / ginning and the end."

Blessed are those who do God's commandments,
that they may have the right to the tree of life,
  and may enter the / city through the gates.

"*I*, Jesus, have sent my angel to you,
  with this testimony for / <u>all</u> the churches.

"*I am* the root and the offspring of David,
  I am the / <u>bright</u> morning star."

"*Come!*" say the Spirit and the Bride;
  "Come!" let each / <u>hear</u>-er reply!

Come forward, you who are thirsty,
  let those who desire take the water of / <u>life</u> as a gift.

Setting: Monte Mason © 2004 Monte Mason.
Used by permission. All rights reserved.

174 Canticle P: *A Song of the Spirit*

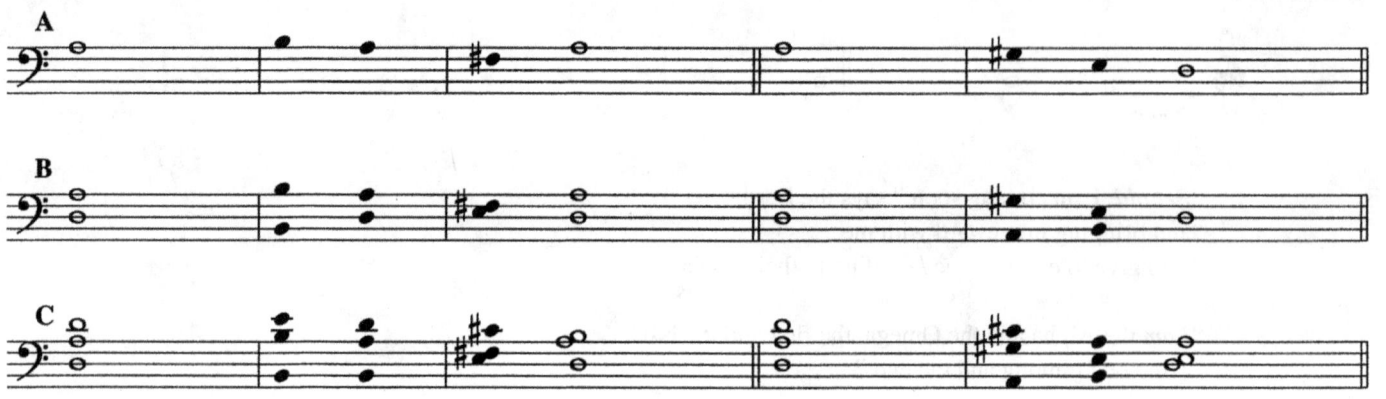

A "Behold, I am coming soon," says the Lord,
"and bringing / my re-ward / with me,
to give to everyone according / to their deeds. **I**

A "I am the Alpha and the Omega, the / first and / the last,
the beginning / and the end." **II**

A Blessed are those who do God's commandments,
that they may have the right to the / tree of / <u>life</u>,
and may enter the city / through the gates. **III**

B "I, Jesus, have sent my / angel / to you,
with this testimony for / all the churches. **II**

B "I am the root and the / offspring of / David,
I am the bright / morning star." **III**

C "Come!" say the Spirit / and the / <u>Bride</u>;
"Come!" let each hear / er reply! **II**

C Come forward, / you who are / thirsty,
let those who desire take the water of life / as a gift. **IV**

May be sung with one or two added voices, B and C, as indicated. When singing all three parts, they are to be sung by either SA or TB, not both: the doubled octaves lack clarity. Handbell "peals" are indicated by Roman numerals, and are to be rung at the cut-off of the voices. Do not damp.

Handbells

Setting: Monte Mason from the Orthodox Church © 2004 Monte Mason.
Used by permission. All rights reserved.

Canticle Q: *A Song of Christ's Goodness* 175

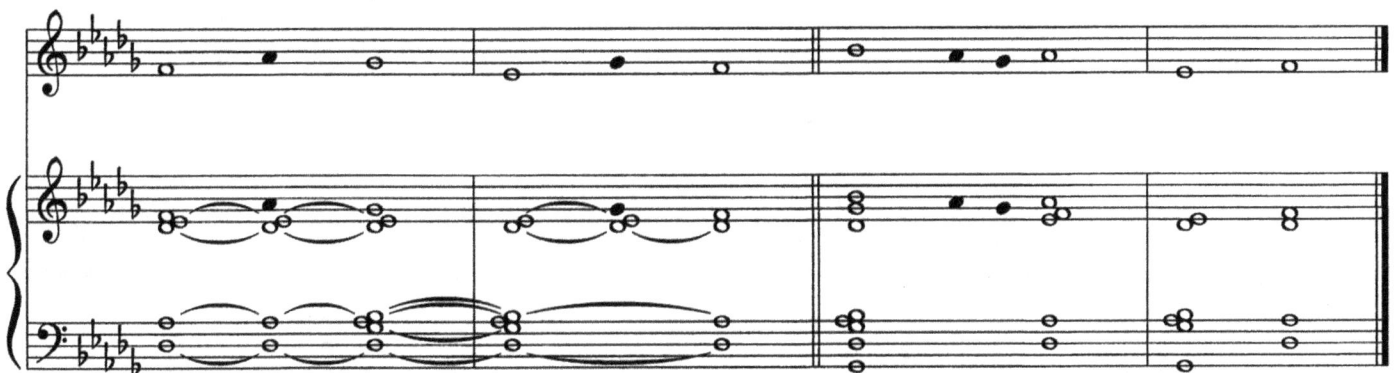

Jesus, as a mother you gather your people / to you;
    you are gentle with us as a mother with / her children.
Often you weep over our sins / and our pride,
    tenderly you draw us from hatred and / judgment.

You comfort us in sorrow and bind up / our wounds,
    in sickness you nurse us and with pure milk / you feed us.
Jesus, by your dying, we are born / to new life;
    by your anguish and labor we come forth in / joy.

Despair turns to hope through your / sweet goodness;
    through your gentleness, we find comfort / in fear.
Your warmth gives life / to the dead,
    your touch makes sinners / righteous.

Lord Jesus, in your mer / cy, heal us;
    in your love and tenderness, / remake us.
In your compassion, bring grace / and forgiveness,
    for the beauty of heaven, may your love pre / pare us.

Setting: George Emblom © 2004 George Emblom.
Used by permission. All rights reserved.

176 Canticle Q: *A Song of Christ's Goodness*

Song of Christ's Goodness - Dimmock

Song of Christ's Goodness - Dimmock

Setting: Jonathan Dimmock © 2002 Jonathan Dimmock.
Used by permission. All rights reserved.

Canticle R: *A Song of True Motherhood* 177

God chose to be our mother in all <u>things</u>
    and so made the foundation of his <u>work</u>,
    most humbly and most <u>pure</u>,
    in the Virgin's <u>womb</u>.

God, the perfect wisdom of <u>all</u>,
    arrayed himself in this humble <u>place</u>.
Christ came in our poor <u>flesh</u>
    to share a mother's <u>care</u>.

Our mothers bear us for pain and for <u>death</u>;
    our true mother, Jesus, bears us for joy and endless <u>life</u>.
Christ carried us within him in love and tra<u>vail</u>,
    until the full time of his <u>passion</u>.

And when all was com<u>pleted</u>
    and he had carried us so for <u>joy</u>,
    still all this could not <u>satisfy</u>
    the power of his wonderful <u>love</u>.

All that we owe is re<u>deemed</u>
    in truly loving <u>God</u>,
    for the love of Christ works <u>in us</u>;
    Christ is the one whom we <u>love</u>.

Setting: Kevin Hacket © 2004 Kevin Hackett.
Used by permission. All rights reserved.

178 Canticle R *A Song of True Motherhood*

A Song of True Motherhood - Martinson

A Song of True Motherhood - Martinson

179 Canticle S: *A Song of Our True Nature*

Song of Our True Nature - Hernández

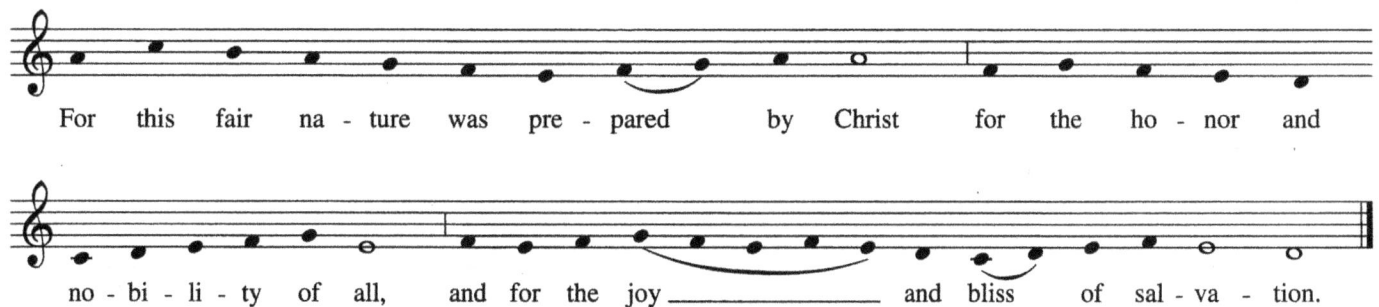

To be sung as chant in a speaking rhythm.

Setting: Ana Hernández © 2004 Ana Hernández.
Used by permission. All rights reserved.

180 Canticle S: *A Song of Our True Nature*

Christ revealed our frailty / and our falling,
  our trespasses and our humil / i-ations.
Christ also revealed his / blessed power,
  his blessed wis / dom and love.

He protects us as tenderly and as sweetly when we are in / greatest need;
  he raises us in spirit
  and turns everything to glory and joy with / out ending.
God is the ground and the substance, the very es / sence of nature;
  God is the true father and mo / ther of natures.

† We are all bound to / God by nature,
  and we are all bound to / God by grace.

And this grace is for / all the world,
  because it is our precious mo / ther, Christ.
For this fair nature was pre / pared by Christ
  for the honor and nobility of all,
  and for the joy and bliss / of salvation.

† *Second half*
Setting: George Emblom © 2004 George Emblom.
Used by permission. All rights reserved.

Title and First Line

A Song of Christ's Goodness	175, 176
A Song of Christ's Humility	165, 166
A Song of Faith	167, 168
A Song of God's Love	169, 170
A Song of Our True Nature	179, 180
A Song of the Heavenly City	171, 172
A Song of the Spirit	173, 174
A Song of True Motherhood	177, 178
All gracious God	137
Alleluia, alleluia	120, 121
Alleluia. Christ is Risen	94
Alleluia. Christ our Passover	141
Be known to us, Lord Jesus	148
Be still and know	151
Behold now, bless the Lord	162
Behold, I am coming soon	173, 174
Beloved, let us love one another	169, 170
Blessed be our God	96
Blessed be the God and Father	167, 168
Blessed be the one	95
Bringing songs of gladness	98
Canticle L	165, 166
Canticle M	167, 168
Canticle N	169, 170
Canticle O	171, 172
Canticle P	173, 174
Canticle Q	175, 176
Canticle R	177, 178
Canticle S	179, 180
Christ has died	134, 135
Christ is arisen! Hallelujah!	157
Christ revealed our frailty	179, 180
Christ, my hope, and Christ, my joy	155
Come, let us sing to the Lord	158, 159
Come, let's be singing	102
Cordero de Dios	145, 146
Day by day we bless you	161
Dying you destroyed our death	135
Eternal Spirit, Life–giver	140
Gloria a Dios	104
Gloria, gloria, gloria	100
Gloria. Gloria in excelsis	99
Glory to God	105
Glory, glory unto you	97
God chose to be our mother	177, 178
God, to my words encline thine ear	153
Hagios, O Theos	117
Halle, halle, hallelujah	119
Hava Hashirah	102
Holy God	118
Holy, holy, holy is the Lord	127

Holy, holy, holy Lord	125, 126, 127
I saw no temple in the city	171, 172
Jesus, as a mother	175, 176
Jubilate Deo	101
Kirisuto no heiwa	150
Kyrie eleison	106, 107, 108, 109
Lamb of God	143, 144
Lamb, O Lamb of God	142
Let my prayer be set forth	163
Live in charity	149
Lord, have mercy	111, 112, 113, 114
Meditation No. 10	152
Meditation No. 9	151
My spirit is longing	156
Now, Lord, you let your servant go	164
O come to my heart, Lord Jesus	154
O God, be merciful to us	161
O God, you are my God	160
O Lord, I call to you	163
Our Father in heaven	137, 138
Sanctus, Sanctus, Sanctus	124
Santo, Santo Dios	116
Santo, santo, santo es el Señor	129, 130, 131, 132
Shanti	122
Sing and rejoice	103
The Lord be with you	123
The Lord is my Light	157
Though in the form of God	165, 166
Throughout a life of hardship	128
Ubi caritas	149
We who are many	147
You are beloved	152

Authors, Composers, Arrangers, Sources

Abell, Joseph H., arr.	131
Anselm of Canterbury	175, 176
Anzalo, Raul	162
Anzalo, Raul	169
Anzalo, Raul	169
Avir, Richard	148
Berthier, Jacques	149
Berthier, Jacques	149
Bianchi, Vicente	145
Black, George, (1931-2003) arr.	125, 133
Boles, Frank W.	108, 60, 125
Bridges, Debra Hinson	99, 124
Burdick, Owen	158, 160, 161, 163
Burnam, Jack, harm.	110
Byzantine	133
Campbell, William	97
Caribbean traditional	119
Chávez-Melo, Skinner	115, 130, 146
Cotter, Jim	140
Crisafulli, Peter	105
Dimmock, Jonathan	115, 135, 136, 176
Dimmock, Jonathan, arr.	109
Duckworth, Bonnie	141
Economides, Greg	126
Elliott, Emily Elizabeth Steele (1836-1897)	154
Emblom, George	167, 175, 180
Emery, Jane	112
Feza, Mary F.	131
Garcia, Juan Luis	129
Giles, Randall	117, 122
Godoy, Carlos Mejia	98, 128, 137, 142
Griswold, Frank	148
Hackett, Kevin	177
Hart, Christopher	110
Haskel, Marilyn	159, 170
Hawthorne, Robert, harm.	118
Hebrew Round	102
Herbert, George (1593-1630)	153
Hernández, Ana	140, 151, 152, 179
Hirten, John Karl	143
Hurd, David	164
Hurd, David, adapt	147
I John 4:7-11	169, 170
I Peter 1:3-4, 18-21	167, 168
Julian of Norwich	177, 178, 179, 180
Kucharski, Joseph A.	134
Marinez, Pablo	98, 128, 137, 142
Martinson, Joel	178
Mason, Monte	139, 165, 168, 171
MaultsBy, Carl	95, 96, 107
Milano, Roberto	132

Mode 6	147
Moore, Hunter	94
Morales, Carlos O.	116
Mozart, Wolfgang Amadeus (1756-1791)	121
Mxadana, Gobingca, arr.	120
Orr, Philip	113
Papadakos, Dorothy, harm.	159
Philippians 2:6-11	165, 166
Praetorius, Michael (1571-1621)	101
Psalm 134	162
Psalm 141:1-3, 8 ab	163
Psalm 27:1, 5-8	157
Psalm 63:1-8	160
Psalm 67:1-5	161
Psalm 95:1-7	158, 159
Revelation 21:22-26, 22:1-4	171, 172
Revelation 22:12-17	173, 174
Rimsky-Korsakov, Nicholas (1844-1908)	138
Roberts, William Bradley	153, 154, 155, 156
Russian Orthodox	111
Sanford, Galen	118
Sdeio, Mark, arr.	119
Shiota, Izumi	150
Sosa, Pablo	100
South African	120
Spanish folk song from Taizé	155
Thomas, Lisa Neufeld	123, 144
Traditional Round	103
Vasselli, Stefano	106, 127
Wyse, Eric, harm.	94

Biographies of the Authors, Composers and Arrangers

Joseph H. Abell a contemporary church musician working in the United States.

Raul Anzalo is a church musician in Minneapolis, Minnesota.

Jacques Berthier was the church musician at the Cathedral of Notre Dame in Paris. He is well-known for his compositions for Taizé.

Vicente Bianchi is a well-known South American composer.

George Black (1931-2003) was a contributor to and convenor of the Task Force for the Canadian hymnbook *Common Praise*. He was past president of the Hymn Society in the United States and Canada.

Frank W. Boles is the church musician at St. Paul's Episcopal Church in Indianapolis.

Debra Hinson Bridges is a private piano teacher.

Owen Burdick is the church musician at Trinity Episcopal Church, Wall Street, New York City.

Jack Burnam is the church musician at Immanuel Episcopal Church, Highlands in Wilmington, Delaware.

William Campbell is a composer living in Tucson, Arizona. He has led music for churches, conferences, and retreats.

Jim Cotter is an ordained member of the Church of Wales and is a wordsmith, lecturer, and retreat leader who is also head of Cairns Publications.

Peter Crisafulli is the church musician at All Saints' Church in Chevy Chase, Maryland.

Jonathan Dimmock is the church musician at St. John's Episcopal Church in Ross, California.

Bonnie Duckworth is a deacon in the Episcopal Church serving the Yadkin Valley Cluster in Salisbury, North Carolina.

Greg Economides is the church musician at St. Francis Episcopal Church, College Station, Texas.

George Emblom is the church musician at St. Mark's Episcopal Church in Berkeley, California.

Jane Emery sings in the choir at the Episcopal Church of St. James the Less in Madison, Tennessee, and teaches public school music.

Juan Luis Garcia (1935-1997) was a prolific composer of church music. His work is represented in many denominational hymnals.

Randall Giles is the Director of the Department of Music and Liturgy of the Madras Diocese in the Church of South India.

Carlos Medjia Godoy is a church musician at Christ Church Cathedral in Vancouver, British Columbia.

Frank T. Griswold is the Presiding Bishop of the Episcopal Church in the United States.

Kevin Hackett directs the music for the Society of St. John the Evangelist in Cambridge, Massachusetts.

Christopher Hart is the Minister of Music serving Heritage United Methodist Church in Broken Arrow, Oklahoma.

Marilyn Haskel is a church musician and music editor in New York City.

Robert Hawthorne is Dean of the Vocal Academy at Southridge High School in Beaverton, Oregon, and has served the Episcopal Church for eleven years.

Ana Hernández is a free-lance composer, arranger, and recording artist who also leads workshops in the Episcopal Church.

John Karl Hirten is the church musician at St. Stephen's Episcopal Church in Belvedere, California.

David Hurd is Professor of Music and Chapel Organist at the General Theological Seminary in New York.

Joseph A. Kucharski is Canon Precentor at All Saints Cathedral in Milwaukee.

Pablo Martinez is a church musician at Christ Church Cathedral in Vancouver, British Columbia.

Joel Martinson is the church musician at the Episcopal Church of the Transfiguration in Dallas.

Monte Mason is the church musician at St. Martin's-by-the-Lake in Minnetonka Beach, Minnesota.

Carl MaultsBy is the church musician at St. Mark's Episcopal Church in Brooklyn, New York.

Skinner Chávez Melo (1944-1992) was a church musician, composer, and arranger.

Roberto Milano is a professor at the Conservatory of Music of Puerto Rico.

Hunter Moore is a performing songwriter living and working in Nashville who borrows from country, folk, and blues.

Carlos R. Morales is a contemporary composer of church music in Puerto Rico.

Gobingca Mxadana is a contemporary musician from South Africa.

Philip Orr is church musician at Calvary Baptist Church, Hopewell, New Jersey, and adjunct assistant professor of theory at Westminster Choir College.

Mary F. Reza is a contemporary church music composer working in the United States.

William Bradley Roberts is the church musician at St. John's Episcopal Church, Lafayette Square, Washington, D.C.

Galen Sanford is a high school student at Lakeridge High School and a member of Christ Episcopal Church in Lake Oswego, Oregon.

Mark Sedio is Cantor at Mount Olive Lutheran Church in Minneapolis, Minnesota.

Izumi Shiota is a priest in Japan.

Pablo Sosa is an Argentinian hymn writer and social activist.

Lisa Neufeld Thomas is the Director of the Women's Sacred Music Project in Philadelphia.

Stefano Vasselli is the church musician at St. Paul's Within the Walls in Rome, Italy.

Eric Wyse is the church musician at St. Bartholomew's Episcopal Church in Nashville.

Copyrights

Acknowledgment

Every effort has been made to determine the owner and/or administrator of copyrighted material in the book and to obtain the necessary permission. After given written notice, the Publisher will make the necessary correction(s) in subsequent printings.

Permissions

The Publisher gratefully acknowledges all the copyright holders who have permitted the reproduction of their materials in this book. We especially thank those who have consented to allow Church Publishing to issue one-time, not-for-profit use free of charge. You must contact Church Publishing in writing to obtain this permission (see contact information below).

Certain selections will note those copyright holders who require that you contact them directly to obtain permission to reprint their materials, and their contact information is listed on page 149.

For extended or for-profit use of copyrighted materials in this book, you must write directly to the copyright holder. Contact Church Publishing for information.

Church Publishing Incorporated
19 East 34th Street
New York, NY 10016
Email: churchpublishing@cpg.org

Augsburg Fortress Publishers
P.O. Box 1209
Minneapolis, MN 55440
Phone: 1-800-421-0239
Fax: 1-612-330-3252
E-mail: copyright@augsburgfortress.org
Web: www.augsburgfortress.org

GIA Publications Inc.
7404 South Mason Avenue
Chicago, IL 60638
Phone: 1-800-442-1358
Fax: 1-708-496-3828
E-mail: reprints@giamusic.com
Web: www.giamusic.com

Maulted Milk Music
Carl MaultsBy
575 Riverside Drive, 51
New York, NY 10031
Phone: 1-212-368-7117
E-mail: albany512@yahoo.com

Oregon Catholic Press
P.O. Box 18030
Portland, OR 97218
Phone: 1-800-548-8749
Fax: 1-503-282-3486
E-mail: liturgy@ocp.org
Web: www.ocp.org

www.ingramcontent.com/pod-product-compliance
Lightning Source LLC
Chambersburg PA
CBHW080225170426
43192CB00015B/2754